# EMBRACING
# the UNFORESEEN
## *Improvisation in life and faith*

## Dennis Plies

General editor: Daniel Colvin
Photography and design: Howard Whitaker

# Dedication

Dedicated to my one and only, Barb, whom I met in 1963 and one year later married. She is an amazing person with supreme faith in God and in people; a knock-out improviser in conversation, flower arranging, cooking, and hospitality; and a devoted companion on life's path. She provides me with emotional support, allowing me freedom to read, think, and write. Her tending to the details of life, the practical matters for which I'm close to zero in ability and attitude, have created space and time, allowing me to commit to the book in the first place.

# Contents

# Acknowledgments

With a book promoting collaboration comes an automatic expectation that such a model will be followed, if only for the sake of integrity. For me this is not a problem, for it is my working style. If one of my gifts or natural tendencies is encouraging others, another of my traits is networking and identifying persons for common goals. I get great satisfaction from connecting the right persons for their goals and I am more than satisfied to stay out of their way. Applied to my project of researching and assembling this book, I have relied on many friends. For me that is like breathing.

The following were co-thinkers along the way and/or readers, and in all cases significant for their import to the book. Some scrutinized with red, green, or black ink on hard copy; some had editing comments through digital means. What I received from these wonderfully supportive experts was vital input. Listed in alphabetical order are those from whom I received counsel and feedback: Kelly Ballard, Steven Barry, Irv Brendlinger, Brad Cullen, Cole Dawson, Bill Dobrenen, Sammy Epstein, Lou Foltz, Harold Gray, Joe Hertzberg, Jamil Kassab, Arthur Kelly, Kent Layden, Gary Miniszewski, Derek Moyer, Art Nanna, Jeannine Nordlund, Dean Ober, Luke Pederson, Matt Plies, Walter Saul, Jeff Sweeney, Bryan Williams, and Mary Zinkin.

An exceptional amount of sideline support for this project has come from Howard Whitaker. I recall one recent summer when he was visiting from the midwest, mainly to hang out, listen to music together, hike, and mostly to converse as we can for hours, yet I had this weight of having written the three chapters on dialogue and he helped me sentence by sentence, paragraph by paragraph to get the writing up one more notch. Howard became my objective eyes and mind. Then because of his extraordinary talent for visual art, he kindly consented to my invitation to take and determine the photograph that can begin to capture the concept of the unforeseen and to oversee all the graphic portions of the book. His contributions to this project and his friendship mean the world to me.

And now for the punch line. I have been able to work collaboratively with my close friend, Dan Colvin, including the earliest months discussing my initial research for this book. Though Dan lives in Illinois and I live in Oregon, we have done our very best to get together yearly since 1978. His willingness the past few years to converse heavily within the subject matter of the book as it developed has provided me with joy and confidence to keep going. Dan, a Shakespeare scholar and professor, yields over-the-top ability to move with the crazy notions I assert concerning faith, improvisation, and dialogue. This journey of over seven years, absorbing Dan's input through his sparring, questioning, and in general working with me toward formulating what the book has become, has meant more to me than I can express. I am deeply indebted and fiercely thankful to him for dedicating innumerable hours to the editing process over the past two years. Within his role as editor we have become even better friends. That speaks volumes, for Dan and I agreed that his suggestions would not be tamed, nor would they override my heart and motivation for what I am saying. I can report that through the process of hundreds of hours of serious work together we both exhibited trust and respect toward one another, and our friendship is even deeper and more joyous. Dan, again, heaps of gratefulness to you!!

# How to Use This Book

This book comes out of my own experiences and is grounded in my own thinking. Still, I hope that you will find your own journey in mine. I share these anecdotes and thoughts with you because I believe you will see much of your life in mine, and that together we can examine our adventures.

Although this book can be read by an individual, all along I have intended this project to be one in which a small group could form and agree to meet regularly (weekly, bi-weekly, monthly) for nine sessions. Between meetings each person would be expected to read the chapter and consider the questions, which are meant as prompts. They can be used at the group's pleasure, not compulsively trying to get through all of them. Using the ones that members of the group want to explore provides natural energy for discussion. Actually, as long as the group is having a significant conversation, even questions or prompts created by group members would serve the purposes just as well. The point is to have meaningful conversation concerning substantive life issues. I believe that a group will be more effective if it is held together by relationships than if it is held together by a topic.

A group should have a leader rather than a teacher, one who knows how to listen to others, one who may be considered an initiator-facilitator. The group will not profit from any type of heavy-handed command, but rather a one-of-the-group type of person who can begin, sustain, and truncate conversation, all for the sake of the entire group. That same person can schedule and notify everyone of calendar expectations and lead decision-making toward any food/drink inclusion. Everything should be consensual and amiable.

I have culled the following suggestions from my experience and from my readings, and they are offered as guidelines for group process. It's recommended that all members, not only the leader, keep one another accountable to these expectations. Not to be viewed as rules, these understandings can make everyone's time more worthwhile for the purpose the group meets in the first place.

- ❖ Listen to understand, not to fix, save, advise or set each other straight.
- ❖ Keep each other at task.
- ❖ If the quality of the conversation degenerates, cleverly restore the level without inducing guilt.
- ❖ Allow others to express feelings freely.
- ❖ Exhibit empathy; have compassion for each other and sensitivity to the context.
- ❖ Wonder about something instead of defending something.
- ❖ Be sure everyone participates and no one dominates.
- ❖ Push toward equal time; take turns speaking, allowing everyone's voice to be heard.
- ❖ Keep comments to the point so everyone has a chance to share.
- ❖ Use "I" statements as much as possible.
- ❖ Be open, willing to be influenced.
- ❖ Practice equality: I respect you and therefore the validity of your position.
- ❖ Apply respect. Give everyone the right to his or her opinion; encourage and respect all questions. Pay attention to the person sharing without disrupting or talking to someone else.

# Introduction

Increasingly we live in a fast-paced world, seemingly connected and driven to feel united with innumerable persons through social media, yet many of us are downright lonely and depressed. Templates abound and must be followed. While there is great freedom in such precise structures, the human heart also yearns for flexibility. Sometimes clear, precise communication does the job, but there are other times when we long for contextualization. There is a time for quantifiable descriptions, yet there are times we crave qualifiable discourse. With intercultural communication increasing, the call beckons for even more flexibility as we attempt to interact with diverse perspectives. Recognizing our rapidly changing world and therefore increased needs of adaptability, I decided to write this book to show the cohesion of faith, improvisation, and dialogue. Ultimately I hope to produce a paradigm for freeing creativity.

The project began when I observed parallels between improvisation and faith, but it soon grew to include dialogue. It appears that what transpires in one of these areas resides within the other two. All three of the terms—faith, improvisation, dialogue—presuppose relationships. This book explores ways in which freedom relates to discipline within boundaries and how it is possible to thrive in the tension between freedom and constraints, or, structured creativity, disciplined imagination.

For a three-year-old, playing in the middle of a busy street might seem like life without boundaries, yet it does not culminate in freedom. Somehow a responsible parent must find a way to provide appropriate restraints for the child. How much does a parent steer, follow, and accompany a child? Freedom exhibits profound paradox.

I'm deeply passionate about making music and performance. Until I was about thirty I performed classical pieces in public, having been taught and coached by professional overseers. This brought about a sense of freedom for me. I cannot forget the day, however, when I performed a piece by J. S. Bach that I had learned without outside coaching. I performed for an audience of sophisticated music teachers. They loved my interpretation and musicianship. What a rite of passage for me. That was a newfound freedom, in a different form. I then developed more faith in myself.

Fear of imperfection and/or negative judgment from others can keep us from being our authentic selves. Living to prevent keeps us from learning through our mistakes and developing our potential. But when we see ourselves as we truly are and accept ourselves, we are free to grow. This book addresses our ways of seeing and our ways of being in order to stimulate meaningful thinking, particularly toward sharing in intentional small groups and with your friends informally along the path of life. Good friend Ted Nordlund helps persons become all they can be—fully alive, authentic, loving themselves as well as others. He says, "Spiritual transformation cannot be orchestrated or controlled, but neither is it a random venture. We need some kind of support or structure much like a young vine needs a trellis. We need sails to help us catch the wind of the Spirit." This speaks of structure, freedom, letting go of control, and improvisation. It is catching the power of that which cannot be perceived or necessarily seen.

Admittedly jazz symbolizes much of what I present in this book. Jazz is spontaneous, inventive, and expressive. As a social process in which collaboration moves toward a credible and aesthetically pleasing outcome, the jazz process is based on the premise that each individual is simultaneously adapting to the whole while contributing mutual support and influence. This is faith in oneself, the other, improvisation, and dialogue.

As humans we have in common the capacity and need for meaning. I invite you to connect the word *faith* with *meaning*. Faith will be addressed in this book holistically, even when seemingly pointed in a religious or spiritual direction. The intention is for faith to create meaning.

I'm placing faith in you to read the word "faith" with this openness, not circumscribed by often-used limitations. In this way human faith is active, dynamic, courageous, and unquestionably relational. And relationships are central to meaning.

## *Part One*
# Confluence and Faith

# CHAPTER ONE

# *My Relational Faith Journey*

Because faith can be understood so differently in different contexts—and sometimes in inflammatory ways—I think that a preamble will help to engage your full attention rather than lose it.

The matter of "faith" raises a whole range of questions. Does faith always have to be religious? Does it excite only spiritual outcomes—religion, church, or God? Does it have to mean the opposite of reason? Admittedly this word has many emotional associations and many strong connections emerge, directly and indirectly, because of those connotations and because it is thrown around so freely and loosely. It can have limited, even parochial meanings—and, although more rarely applied, it can also have a more universal application. While I am comfortable using it in its "religious" sense, I am not constrained by that restriction. I maintain that everyone has faith in something or someone that generates a sense of meaning and purpose.

This book, then, is a means toward an end. I want to talk about faith in the context of my experience, not because my story is important in itself but rather because it is a way for dialogue between you, the reader, and me. I hope that in that dialogue we will both begin to define, develop, and appreciate more fully the journey we are on.

Because faith involves loyalty and love, it can be experienced by all who can express loyalty and love relationally. If, for example, faith means being true to someone, faith becomes much more universally positive and interpersonal; it is removed from the ideological and political realm. Even though this chapter may strike you as religious, my intent is to be neither persuasive nor pushy. While I am honestly passionate and direct about this exploration, I want simply to narrate my own faith story in a way that explicitly encourages you to reflect on your own journey. My journey happens to be expressed most meaningfully spiritually, so in order for me to be authentic it is with that voice I must write. I want only to invite and encourage. All of us have faith in the rother/others/Other who help us construct meaning and develop purpose in life.

I realize that I initially identified and practiced faith knowingly through what is traditionally considered a "religious" experience. In fact, I am practicing faith all through the day in manners and matters that many would not consider religious. When I exercise, eat, sleep, travel, read, socialize, experience aesthetic events, and in general determine how I spend time and money, I am applying faith, something beyond belief. If I choose selected exercises, it's because I have faith that they would be enjoyable or worthwhile. When I settle on where to go for a travel experience, in what am I applying faith: the travel agent, my own research, hearsay from others, advertisements? All of these examples have relational elements built in via either persons or other media. Aware of faith applied constantly, my choice is to share my spiritual pilgrimage, for in it I can best represent my understanding of faith and its ubiquitous nature to all of life.

*Faith has to do with what the mind
cannot grasp.
Faith is beyond understanding.*

Realizing that we do not concoct our faith journey, but rather it develops naturally, we can reflect on and own what has transpired. In retrospect, we can see that there were times when we acted without reason or evidence, times when we experienced the mystery of existence as part of the process. Looking back, we can see how the parts fit together into the whole, a whole we could not perceive at the time. We understand now what we could not fathom then. Faith has to do with what the mind cannot grasp. Faith is beyond understanding. From the New Testament we learn that "Faith is the confidence that what we hope for will actually happen; it gives us assurance about things we cannot see." (Hebrews 11:1)

Our daily experience reveals to us that we live in a world of opposites, of tensions. We want to lose weight, but we love that dessert. We know we need to get that task done, but we find the television calling to us. We know that a used minivan would suit our family needs perfectly, but find ourselves buying the sports car. We discover that part of us functions at the level of reason, and part of us functions at another level.

But there is another duality that is just as real as the reason/emotion split. There is the world of perceived reality, and there is also the world of an unseen existence. We see the flower, but unseen to us are the atoms that form it, though we know those atoms are there somehow. We see the violence of rebellions and wars, but we don't see the emotional, psychological, and spiritual factors involved.

What we are experiencing, I think, is the conundrum of human experience, the interweaving of our physical and non-physical natures. We find that the reason and the senses can deal with only one part of that reality; something beyond them is needed to grasp the other—the spiritual or non-physical—world we inhabit.

This duality shapes much of my consideration of what I will present as my relational faith journey. Not based on reasons, my faith in God has to do with an inner awareness of divinity. I find that faith is first embodied non-intellectually. I have found faith to be meaningful within my awareness of God, which looks much different than a constant struggle with God. Daniel Taylor goes another step: "Faith, however, is not a matter of rolling the dice. It is, or can be, a conscious expression of a great gift—human freedom. God has given us all the ability to either choose or reject a relationship with Him." Here is my story of meaning and fulfillment with the hope that you will reflect seriously on your story.

When I was seven, I became aware of God's forgiveness because I saw that Jesus came to earth to die sacrificially not only for all humanity, past and future, but also for me, for what I was as a sinner but also for the sins I had committed. Jesus as a human had God-faith, practicing a continual awareness of God's presence. This was a relationship demonstrating to all humanity that this was also possible for us to be connected to our Source. And being connected to the Source, God, summarizes my purpose in life.

Looking backward to this heart decision to receive God's forgiveness means that I then, as now, was aware of a fractured relationship with my Maker. Separation from the Source is how I am describing the old-fashioned word "sin." My friend Irv Brendlinger states, "Sin is being less than we were created to be and not fulfilling what God designed us for. It is not a list of behaviors we have done or a list of rules (laws) we have broken. These are the results of sin." Sin is hiding from God. Sin is forgetting that I am created by God. Sin is failing to grow. Sin is running from my shadow, not dealing with my darkness. Sin hurts other people. Sin is a form of self-abuse. Sin shows itself as pride, isolating the self, aborting the possibility of friendship. This then affects larger masses of people through colonization, slavery, racism, sexism, indifference to the poor, addiction, and scapegoating. All of these images coalesce in the self-centered nature of sin. The Hebrew word generally translated as sin is "het," which comes from the word in archery meaning "to miss the mark." In feeling the reality of sin as described by any of the above examples, I accept God's forgiveness through faith. In the words of Nels F. S. Ferré, "As Savior, Jesus shows us our sin both of self and of society. The light shows up the dark. Unless we can see what is wrong with us, we are unwilling to be made right. How dark sin is, was not seen until Jesus lived."

Another story illustrates how forgiveness can be practiced as a lifestyle. For about thirty years I carried a heavy grudge toward someone. All that time I had legitimized my bitterness, not realizing how foolish it was. Because the feelings were strong and I had sufficient cause through my reasoning power to hold onto my petty grievance, the resentment persisted. Then one evening when teaching a four-hour class I closed by sharing a particular challenge with my students. I mentioned that it may seem that each of us has a distinct vocation, whether lived out as a manager, electrician, social worker, salesperson, lawyer, engineer or whatever, but that there was another way to look at vocation. Reminding them that "vocation" meant that to which we are called, I suggested that we are all given the call to reconciliation, something all of us could practice every day.

On my way home I suddenly remembered what I had said to the class. I realized that the next day I would be with the person against whom I held such ill will. I also realized that I wanted to keep my vindictive attitude—after all, I was in the right! Emotionally gripped, I was moved immediately to tell God that my heart was ready to be forgiving and to live the way God always models love. Instantly I sensed freedom and a loving, advocating spirit toward this person. Healing had taken place. I had presented awareness of my shortcoming and egocentric attitude to my Maker as an act of surrender. In letting go I knew that the relationship was re-paired. My experience in the car had a vital and lifelong effect on my heart—I was able to accept the other person without reservation.

I believe that what is common to all religious faith traditions is compassion. In the Christian tradition this love is shown through complete forgiveness, so that when Jesus was dying on the cross, his response was "Father, forgive them; for they know not what they do." Reinhold Niebuhr broadens that statement by putting it in the context of being "saved": "Nothing that is worth doing can be achieved in our lifetime; therefore, we must be saved by hope. Nothing that is true, or beautiful, or good, makes complete sense in any immediate context of history; therefore, we must be saved by faith. Nothing we do, however virtuous, could be accomplished alone; therefore, we must be saved by love. No virtuous act is quite as virtuous from the standpoint of our friend or foe as it is from our own standpoint; therefore, we must be saved by the final form of love, which is forgiveness."

After my initial decision to accept God's forgiveness, I continued my journey by memorizing Bible verses and learning a great deal about how to live a Christian life. The pure experience of love and forgiveness eventually became tempered by the Christian culture in which I was living, as community mores became increasingly normative for me. A community seeking to know Jesus and His love is poles apart from a community based mostly on American Christian culture. When faith is solely in Jesus's life as model, I seek the best for the other person. I'm all about focusing on forgiving love instead of a set of beliefs and behaviors. Dogma brings about parochialism, conformity, exclusion, and coercion. I want, rather, to pursue love as the emphasis, in fact, the full message. Carol Gilligan, known for her "Ethics of Care," expresses love this way: "The ideal of care is thus an activity of relationship, of seeing and responding to need, taking care of the world by sustaining the web of connection so that no one is left alone."

By the time I reached my teen years I realized that I was working very hard defending my religious beliefs. My faith persisted, yet it was getting muddled. By attempting to be virtuous and trying to prove others wrong in order for me to feel right, I found myself trying to persuade others to agree with me. This was a result of my reasoning. Instead of relishing the experience of forgiveness and learning all I could about the truth and power of forgiveness, I was busy putting people straight on how to believe and behave. I had the "correct" package and I was serious about others having the same package. I was intellectualizing my understanding of truth. Rather than following the practice of faith, I was on a detour, a path of mixed meaning. Had I continually tuned into my initial forgiveness theme, I would have experienced much more freedom and peace.

Some see faith as "one way." Some see faith as giving the strength to welcome the diversity and challenge of other perspectives. Some see the challenge of different beliefs and experiences as an opportunity to grow. Others see a violation of their own truth—an attack on the core of their being. Had I truly focused on my faith experience of forgiveness, I would have been able to welcome the various perspectives of others. In my most mature moments I hope that I am simply thankful for the revelation I do have and hope to be free to listen to the narratives of others. All the while I want to live the love model of Jesus.

Like many young people, I found that society began having a significant influence on my thinking and behavior. Agonizingly wanting to know what was right and worrying about getting my theology straight seemed to be the order of the day in my early twenties. I was frustrated and caught as if inside a cage. At the same time I could not articulate my problem. Without knowing it, I wanted deliverance but had no inkling of how to get freed without tossing the baby out with the bath water. I sought truth through reading, conversing, grumbling, and thinking. As I look back on those years, I realize that my persistence to find truth via thinking meant I was bound to miss what I was after. By trusting my thinking I was losing my initial empowering experience of loving forgiveness as the way—through faith. Now I see how clearly this predicament is articulated in Proverbs 3:5-6: "Trust in the LORD with all your heart and lean not on your own understanding; in all your ways submit to him, and he will make your paths straight." The role of knowledge and the role of faith can be at odds when one depends on knowledge rather than on the Source of knowledge.

In my twenties I began deconstructing my worldview in order to construct a new one that would better reflect the reality I was experiencing. One of the ways I did this occurred in my own mind. I imagined that I was on an island, all alone, reading the Bible. My challenge was to decipher what it meant without the prodding of others. What I didn't realize, however, was that I was limited by depending on only my head and not my heart. I needed a better way to find where faith and meaning intersected.

## *Because all humans want to construct meaning in their lives, faith is a universal necessity.*

Because all humans want to construct meaning in their lives, faith is a universal necessity. The soul can live without success, but it cannot live without meaning. Early life experiences and added confusing issues made me determined to find what was ultimately true and dependable, what could help me construct meaning in my life. In her study of this

stage of life's journey, Sharon Daloz Parks writes, "Though faith has become problematic, the importance of meaning has not. William G. Perry
Jr., who has contributed so much to our understanding of meaning-
making in young adulthood, often remarked that the purpose of an or-
ganism is to organize, and what human beings organize is meaning.
Meaning-making is the activity of composing a sense of the connections
among things: a sense of pattern, order, form, and significance. To be human is to seek coherence and correspondence. To be human is to want to
be oriented to one's surroundings. To be human is to desire relationship
among the disparate elements of existence."

When I was twenty-six I was fortunate to receive a major enlight-
enment when I met Don Alexander. The first time I encountered him I
was struck by his warm and genuine smile; even more significant was
the way he spoke with me, a manner that expressed unconditional love
and real care for me. Don asked me many questions; consequently, we
established weekly study sessions poring over the book of Romans with
a heavy dose of Karl Barth's influence. After a few weeks of invigorated
thinking and experiencing Jesus through Don's modeling and mentoring,
I began to get it. The result became a change in my personal foundation
of meaning-making from needing to understand and interpret the scriptures correctly to simply enjoying the person of Jesus, the Christ. I found
the scriptures pointed me to Jesus. This basis for faith in the person of
Jesus was much more relational in the sense of person to Person, spirit
to Spirit. Jesus had walked this life on earth for 33 years. Jesus cared for
humans, enough to have come, agonized, suffered, died, and been resur-
rected. The heart of this Good News was His sacrifice evidenced on the
Cross, demonstrating a forgiving spirit with no resentment, even while
dying. What a model of relinquishing control!

To get a sense of how revolutionary pure love is, consider an opposite form. Donald McCullough states, "Suicide is the pursuit of death,
the attempt to take death into our own hands, and it is, in a paradoxical
way, simply another effort to escape the pain of limitations. The surrender we're called to is far more radical; it is a release of our control, an

acceptance of life and all its limitations, a falling, not happily but willingly, into something too dark to see but what we fear may be Nothing. There is only one way to do this, I believe: trusting the One who speaks to us from the far side of death." To pursue the way of life is to eschew control, accept limitations, and actively forgive both others and ourselves.

With the combination of my early faith experience and this renewal through meeting Don Alexander, I was now not banking on my brain for faith. Imagine someone who had read of the Grand Canyon, perhaps had even seen some pictures, but had never been there encountering it for the first time. The intellectual preparation would fall far short of his actual experience. It's like the person who says, "I once was blind but now I see!" The faith experience is amazing and joyous even without scientific savvy to explain it. Some experiences don't depend on evidence-based knowledge; in some situations, however, intellectual understanding can follow.

Indescribable experiences of faith bring celebration. Parker J. Palmer states, "When Jesus accepted the cross, his death became a channel for the redeeming power of love. When we accept the crosses and contradictions in our lives, we allow that same power to flow." Some experiences leave us speechless, for they are inexplicably profound. Faith experiences are a whole lot more exciting than getting theology all figured out. Yet in the confluence of the rational and the relational, experience is enriched and is exuberant.

Unchanging in this discussion is the relational bent to faith, so liberating and fulfilling. In contrast, a diverting substitute often comes in the form of wanting to believe and behave in the "right" way. Its result is very likely anxiety. The obsession to "know what I believe" can be a setup for worry, for the pressure rests on my figuring it out. If, for example, the concern is the nature and role of prayer, a framed question such as, "Am I praying sufficiently and properly?" is conceivable. Seeing prayer as relationship rather than a rule alters the focus greatly. Mark Labberton says, "Prayer is taking God's invitation to personal relationship at face value. It's neither formulaic nor predictable. It is relationship. It's not about our power but about God's." This distinction is extremely valuable in show-ing how faith works. Only by relying on God's strength, in having faith in the person of God, can our limitations and weaknesses be overcome.

My faith journey had begun in a meaningful experience of love, moved to adhering to rules, struggled through reconstructing my world-view, and found itself in a stance of freedom grounded in experiential love. I believe life's purpose is to embrace God's love through a respon-sible freedom. God's love frees us, but our freedom is limited, limited by our own choice to respond to God as responsible, integrated persons. Love and freedom are inextricably linked; they are interdependent. I re-alize why so many hang onto a lifestyle of dogma, obeying compulsively, for in its black and white nature there is an attraction and a certainty; but the human spirit craves freedom. We misunderstand when we think that following the rules is true love, for that path can lead to phoniness and a lack of authenticity. Merely loving without responsibility leads to chaos and a lack of accountability. In freedom and love there are admit-tedly convoluted, paradoxical components, until we realize the joy and the privilege of making choices.

## *Faith presses us beyond the cognitive limitations of the brain's capacity. . . . faith is relational, interactive, and social.*

Human beings function by faith. We want to know how to put our lives together and what imparts value. James W. Fowler, a specialist on this subject, says, "[F]aith is a person's or group's way of moving into the force field of life. It is our way of finding coherence in and giving mean-ing to the multiple forces and relations that make up our lives. Faith is a person's way of seeing him- or herself in relation to others against a back-ground of shared meaning and purpose." To examine faith as a universal capacity is to appreciate how faith is relational, interactive, and social. As a journey, a process, faith is dynamic, ready to burst a tightly sealed jar, for faith is a verb. Faith presses us beyond the cognitive limitations of the brain's capacity. From being bound, judgmental, critical, and all that signifies control, I believe a more enjoyable and exciting life comes through release to Almighty Spirit. This includes confession, an acceptance of self, and an openness to receive others as they are, knowing that all of us are on a path of "becoming." For me, jazz epitomizes the passion and freedom of which I speak. The improvisation prevalent in jazz expresses the meaning of faith. It's the giving up of control and letting go.

# CHAPTER TWO

# *What Faith Is and Is Not*

Crossing Niagara Falls on a tightrope involves action. It takes faith—beyond belief and understanding—to take that first step, but it also demands a reasoned assessment of skill. Before the walker takes the first step, there is absolute freedom; he is free to step out as well as free to turn around and go home. Once he takes his first step, that act of faith leads him into the encounter with risk, fear, and courage. Finally, after the crossing, the walker experiences the exhilaration of having overcome the challenge and the satisfaction of self-discovery and personal meaning. Faith allows the walker to go beyond logic and act, even though he cannot "see everything."

While faith does not involve certainty, it clearly demands courage, as Paul Tillich suggests: "Faith is certain in so far as it is an experience of the holy. But faith is uncertain in so far as the infinite to which it is related is received by a finite being. This element of uncertainty in faith cannot be removed, it must be accepted. And the element in faith that accepts this is courage. Faith includes an element of uncertainty. To accept this is courage. In the courageous standing of uncertainty, faith shows most visibly its dynamic character." After a child gets her first bicycle, she practices riding using training wheels. Then her parent removes the training wheels and she pedals with her parent holding onto the seat. Finally, after her parents tell her, "You can do this! You are ready," she takes off alone in an act of faith and courage, though uncertain of the ultimate outcome.

Faith has much to do with our core values, those things we believe in most deeply, that we see to be good, that give meaning to our lives. In that sense, most of what we do involves faith, for what we value often determines what we choose. These core values guide our lives, create co-herence for us, and help us act on what we deem to be true. These values, this faith, also help us feel connected, to our world in general but more significantly to others around us, for we find meaning in relationships. Scott Russell Sanders talks about this in relation to marriage. He suggests that in the marriage vow the choosing one and therefore forsak-ing all others gives meaning. In his words, "Fidelity entails restraint." Furthermore, "Marriage gives meaning to desire, gives it a purpose, a history, a home."

Faith embodies many dualities, among them this world and the other world, material and spiritual, inner life and outer action, and natural reason and supernatural faith. When people fall in love, they know that it wasn't analytical reasoning that sparked the romance. Although not necessarily logical, love is nonetheless real and mean-ingful. Somehow the worlds of reason and emotion come together to create one of the most significant human experiences. When it occurs, both persons know it and know that it is beyond understanding. It's sublime. It's other-worldly.

Spiritual faith, like love, goes beyond what sight or reason can com-prehend. According to Frederich Buechner, "Faith is a way of looking at what is seen and understanding it in a new sense. Faith is a way of look-ing at what there is to be seen in the world and in ourselves and hoping, trusting, believing against all evidence to the contrary that beneath the surface we see there is vastly more that we cannot see." In faith, as in love, we experience a mysterious duality that drives us to seek meaning, connectedness, and coherence.

*Belief is a term associated with faith, but it is not in itself faith.*

Belief is a term associated with faith, but it is not in itself faith. Beliefs are powerful, for they lead to decisions. My beliefs are what I give my heart to, and conversely what I give my heart to reveals what I believe. Essentially, belief is a thought structure. My free will is involved, yet an accompanying commitment must follow, with the obvious element of risk included. More than a matter of accepting a certain set of statements, faith has built into it a dynamic expectation of transformation. Faith acts on a belief. Believing my spouse loves me and that she will keep her vows is not sufficient to create a marriage. As Gregory Boyd says, "Believing those things are preconditions for my relationship with her, but they are not themselves the marriage relationship." Marriage is a willingness to act continually in relationship with my spouse, despite uncertainty, doubt, fear, anxiety, failure, and change, a dynamic blending that exhibits the mystery of love.

Belief is an understanding. Faith is not. As I journey through life I am establishing beliefs that guide me. Along the path I realize that my beliefs have come from my culture and my upbringing; therefore, at a certain point, since these accumulated beliefs came from without, not necessarily from within, I need to doubt them and examine them. Only then can my beliefs become truly my own. Philip Yancey illustrates this development of a personal, internal, integrated belief system:

> Kathleen Norris tells of a long intellectual battle against the faith of her childhood, finding it impossible for a time to swallow much of Christian doctrine. Later, experiencing problems in her personal life, she felt drawn to a Benedictine abbey where, to her surprise, the monks seemed unconcerned about her weighty doubts and intellectual frustrations. "I was a bit disappointed," she writes. "I had thought that my doubts were spectacular obstacles to my faith and was confused but intrigued when an old monk blithely stated that doubt is merely the seed of faith, a sign that faith is alive and ready to grow." Rather than address her doubts one by one, the monks instead instructed her in worship and liturgy.

Norris learned that in its Greek root belief means simply "to give one's heart to," and she found that the act of worship can constitute a concrete form of belief. She did not find it strange to recite creeds she could not comprehend, for, as she says, "As a poet I am used to saying what I don't thoroughly comprehend." Gradually it dawned on her that to have a relationship with God, like any relationship, she must plunge into it without knowing where it might take her. She began with trust, and from there a mature faith developed.

## *Without faith it is impossible to function in the world.*

Everyday events in life involve faith. Without faith it is impossible to function in the world. We eat a mushroom in our salad assuming that it is not poisonous. We step on the elevator and push the button, trusting that it will not crash to the basement. We get on the bus and sit next to a stranger, having faith that he will not stab us. We continue to act in these ways, even though we know that sometimes the food is tainted, the elevator falls, or the passenger is demented. We persist despite the possibility we could be wrong. We choose to act in faith.

We can have faith in ourselves, in the stock market, in an invention we think will catch on and be used, in reason, in fatalism, in nonviolence, in hypnotism, or in prayer. From the literal to the conceptual, faith is operative, helping us get through each day. Still, because we are conscious beings, we want to understand how faith fits into everything else; we desire explanations for the deepest questions of life: Why are we here? How are we to live? Realizing that to have purpose suggests an act of faith, we persist in exploring causes and meaning. John Tarrant places these ideas in the context of Buddhist thought: "In a Buddhist sensibility, this ultimacy might be described as Sunyata, usually translated as 'emptiness.'

This use of the word is intended to convey a consciousness of the very foundation of the universe, the vast 'mystery underlying even darkness— from which the earth itself with its mountains, oceans, buildings, animals, people, and clouds is born.'"

To acknowledge the mystery of the universe in relation to faith is not sufficient, however. There must be an operative component to faith. Sharon Daloz Parks says, "Faith is intimately related to doing. We human beings act in accordance with what we really trust—in contrast to what we may merely acclaim. We act in alignment with what we finally perceive as real, oriented by our most powerful centers of trust (or mistrust). Thus our acts, powered by a deeper faith, often belie what we say (or even think) we believe. Our faith is revealed in our behavior." We apply our heart to that which we consider to be true. According to this, faith always has to be practiced.

Martin Luther King, Jr. put his faith on the line. He was pledged to the practice of nonviolence. He saw violence as immoral and impractical; thus he applied faith in the spiritual, expressed by the power of love over hate. In so doing he exemplified the phrase "putting yourself in trouble" as a description of faith. It required determination to believe beyond his doubts. It required a decision. It demonstrated energy and commitment. As an example of faith in action, he lived into expectancy. His faith was about seeking and persevering. He invested his heart and his actions in that which he considered to be true.

Anna Halpin found a focus for her faith in the world of dance. She says, "I have a tremendous faith in the process of a human mechanism, and in creativity as an essential attribute of all human beings. . . .This faith in the process is the only goal or purpose I need." For that matter, "trust in the process" is a mantra of therapists and consultants as well as many teachers. Halpin found that her relationship with her dancers freed them to explore and to discover, and that faith always implies a relationship, one in which the freedom to question is essential. In that context, faith is grounded in the one in whom the faith is invested. Faith may not know where it will lead, but it knows, and trusts, the one who is doing the leading. Anna Halpin focuses on process, and in observing how that works, she can determine levels of reliance each individual dancer has in her and in the process. It's what drives her.

Frederick Buechner sees faith affecting, even infecting, every area of life:

> Faith is different from theology because theology is reasoned, systematic, and orderly, whereas faith is disorderly, intermittent, and full of surprises. Faith is different from mysticism because mystics in their ecstasy become one with what faith can at most see only from afar. Faith is different from ethics because ethics is primarily concerned not, like faith, with our relationship to God but with our relationship to each other. Faith is closest perhaps to worship because like worship it is essentially a response to God and involves the emotions and the physical senses as well as the mind, but worship is consistent, structured, single-minded and seems to know what it's doing while faith is a stranger and exile on the earth and doesn't know for certain about anything. Faith is homesickness. Faith is a lump in the throat. Faith is less a position on than a movement toward, less a sure thing than a hunch. Faith is waiting. Faith is journeying through space and through time.

For Buechner, faith is a human, relational response that comes from a personal source that is beyond reason, mysticism, or ethics; faith is personal.

Such faith is childlike and simple in the best sense. Anneka Prigodich, a ten-year-old, tells her story, one that illustrates the core of the faith we have been exploring. She says, "I was about five years old when I asked the Lord Jesus Christ into my heart. My mom and I were driving to some clothing store and I asked her, 'Mom, can I ask Jesus into my heart like they've been saying at church?' My mom said, 'I suppose, if that's really what you want to do.' So I did. I closed my eyes and said to God, 'God? I've decided that I want to ask you into my heart. Could you please come into it?' And you know what? I may not have known it then, but looking back, I know He has been there ever since, washing away my sins and clothing me in clean, white robes."

Anneka's story is paradigmatic for us. Such simple and beautiful faith can be practiced continually if we live in humility and dependence. Assuming the context is relatively healthy and stable, a child has no doubts about where the next meal will come from. A child goes to school and returns to comfortable security that someone will be there to love her and care for her. That trust is implied in Jesus' instruction to his followers: "People were also bringing babies to Jesus for him to place his hands on them. When the disciples saw this, they rebuked them. But Jesus called the children to him and said, 'Let the little children come to me, and do not hinder them, for the kingdom of God belongs to such as these. Truly I tell you, anyone who will not receive the kingdom of God like a little child will never enter it.'" (Luke 18:15-17)

What Martin Luther King, Jr., Anna Halpin, Frederich Buechner, and Anneka Prigodich have in common is that they all found a focus outside of themselves for faith—the power of nonviolence, the human body in movement, God as the supreme Spirit of Love, or the indwelling forgiving God. In all these cases, meaning and significance came as a result of relating to that focus and committing to it. Faith can be seen not in what we say we believe but in how we act, what we spend our money on, and how we use our time. There is interdependence within a faith relationship. In this relationship we create meaning and discover that faith is ultimately what we set our hearts on.

An excellent illustration of faith was that lived out by Abraham. The writer of Hebrews in the New Testament interprets the story of Abraham in terms of the faith we have been considering: "By faith Abraham, when called to go to a place he would later receive as his inheritance, obeyed and went, even though he did not know where he was going. By faith he made his home in the promised land like a stranger in a foreign country;

he lived in tents, as did Isaac and Jacob, who were heirs with him of the same promise. For he was looking forward to the city with foundations, whose architect and builder is God." (Hebrews 11:8-10) I would think that Abraham would have liked to have known about each step he took and how that would have brought about success and purpose. But Abraham did not and could not have such knowledge. That would do away with the essence of faith. There's an element of reckless willingness to adventure in his narrative. If he had looked for certainty rather than being willing to experience risk, he would not have been living out his faith, and he would not have been listed as one of the heroes in Hebrews 11.

The kind of faith we witness in Abraham runs counter to the kind of controlled, safe, bland experience many seem to find in their own lives. Rather, Abraham's life is a paradoxical, reckless, vicissitudinous journey. Susan K. Williams Smith says, "So faith, crazy faith, is the ability to make the invisible visible and the impossible possible." If it's crazy, then it's primed for adventure. Abraham's journey was all about what could be considered gambling, about giving up control, and essentially being clueless about his future; his reality was beyond his understanding.

Faith houses this craziness and letting go, characteristics not considered necessarily intellectual. Yet Abraham was somehow empowered to experience gratitude as he journeyed. A long-time friend of mine puts it this way: faith is being "utterly grateful for something before experiencing it." Such was Abraham's faith, for he lived in real expectation that what God said was reliable and true. In that he exemplified what the writer of Hebrews says: "And without faith it is impossible to please God, because anyone who comes to him must believe that he exists and that he rewards those who earnestly seek him." (Hebrews 11:6) Once a person determines, or chooses to believe, that the object and source of her faith is reliable and trustworthy, then living by faith becomes nearly effortless, even simple.

In my own case, I'm using as my prime example a spiritual application based on my belief that God is the Source of all life and energy, the "Founder" of existence. Admittedly I cannot prove this; nevertheless, as long as I believe this, I can live by faith in that God. Though I do not know where the journey will take me, I know on whom I lean. Instead of leaning on my own understanding, I lean on Creator God. I declare this leaning as purposeful. Instead of living by my ego or hubris, I choose to live by faith, something I cannot comprehend. I see it as an adventure with unforeseen outcomes.

## *. . . meaning is what we crave, and meaning comes through relationship.*

God did not intend to be completely understood or institutionalized but to be experienced. In America, slaves, when restricted from organized worship, were able to grow in their faith, for they came to God directly, not through the church. That experience of God was unhindered by any strictures. It was relational and it granted meaning. I firmly believe that meaning is what we crave, and meaning comes through relationship. If faith has more to do with the relationship between the subject and the object than about faith per se, then what we are talking about is a dynamic and life-changing relationship. Klyne Snodgrass puts it this way: "Faith is relational, describing reliance on a reliable God. Faith is a covenant word, expressing the commitment and trust that bind two parties together. Throughout Scripture, God by his grace makes promises and commits himself to his people. They in turn are to trust those promises and live in light of them. God shows himself faithful and people are to respond in faithfulness. To say 'I have faith' does not so much say anything about oneself; rather it says, 'God is a trustworthy God.'" What an affirmation of the relational element of faith! Relationships bring about meaning. Whether referring to God in relationship to humans, or humans in relationship to one another, meaning is created.

While intellectually always pursuing truth, I can simultaneously engage faith. Central to that dynamic is my remembering that faith is relational and meaning-making. If, however, I forget that important fact and begin to act as if through my control I could bring about faith and meaning, I soon become arrogant and dispense with faith. Such intellectual reliance would mislead me into a false understanding of myself, of God, and of my relationship to and with God. If I believe I must be responsible mentally for a dynamic relationship, then I'm granting too much value to thinking. Since I'm asserting that what I cannot understand is deemed "faith," then as I live into faith I am free to receive and appreciate further understanding. Rather than needing to prove by understanding, I first place faith in a relationship, thereby gaining freedom to think, the result of faith.

Such an understanding of faith can be shared by those in a group, and it indicates a commonality of vision. An articulation on a welcome brochure of First Presbyterian Church of Berkeley, California, reads, "First Pres is a community thoughtfully engaged in our faith, embracing people of all ages, ethnicities, backgrounds, and circumstances. It is a place where questions can be asked, honest reflection is encouraged, creativity is cultivated, and where faith is not a formula, but a life lived. We seek to be engaged locally and around the world, to listen and to learn, to embody justice and compassion, and to share the love of Jesus Christ in tangible ways as we journey together." To such an intentional communication I feel kinship. I definitely want to experience as much of what they describe as possible. I must highlight the phrase "faith is not a formula, but a life lived."

When I hear accounts of peoples' experiences, their "life lived," especially the stories of their learning, I am inspired. To give an example of a faith experience, I share a story as told by Coren Wilson, one of my former college students, who experienced an unbelievable challenge. She titled it "The Obstacle":

> Challenges and obstacles are part of the human experience. I believe that such obstacles undoubtedly affect one's perception of the world, lifestyle, and future decisions on some level or another.

I know this to be true for myself, as my most recent hardship nearly cost me my life and has subsequently taught me a lot about my faith in God and my need to place all trust in him. The occasion was rather unforeseeable, a beautiful August day marked only by an agenda to have fun with family in the sun and water.

We headed for a nearby river to float in tubes down a section of the river. As we drew near a fork in the river we had to make a decision about which leg to take. We had a mutual agreement that we should head towards the right, but in a minute or so we began to doubt that choice. One of the girls tipped her tube and went under the water, bobbing up a little downstream as she moved in towards the center island in shallow water. My friend Dan and I were further back and it appeared that she was trying to say something to us. By the time we figured out what all the fuss was about neither of us had time to react to the fallen log obstructing our path. In fear I slipped off my tube only to be slammed up against the log. Dan followed in like order.

I hugged onto the tree, my arms straddled on top and bottom as tight as I could possibly grip. The strong current pulled at my legs and I could feel my shoulders being pulled under the water, then my ears. I began screaming for help over and over again. I remembered that we had passed some kayakers who had taken a break not far upriver. My mind raced and my thoughts continued to jump from maintaining my grip on the log to vivid pictures of my body floating lifeless downriver, to my family and friends, who I loved so dearly.

Emotion flooded my body and I began to feel tears well up in my eyes. Amidst all my racing thoughts I heard the voice of God scream, "Coren, SHUT UP, BE

QUIET AND REST!!!" I was transfixed and for a second I felt completely at peace, the water rolling over my shoulders. I prayed for God's protection and for his strength that I so badly needed in this moment. I knew that if I was quiet I would be able to reserve more strength. I pulled my legs toward the tree and straddled the tree with my legs. I looked up and saw the branches of the tree to which I had been completely oblivious before. Slowly and mechanically I grabbed the branch full fisted and pulled myself up so that I was now straddling the log and the majority of my body was out of water.

I noticed two men (the kayakers) downstream who had linked arms, waist deep in water and I began to cry. Now atop the tree I was greatly afraid of leaving. It took a minute or two of persuasion and continuous prayer, but I pushed off and pulled up my legs as to ensure that I wouldn't get caught on any branches underwater. As soon as I was near enough I latched onto one of the gracious strangers and began to sob.

I thank God often for his grace on the river and realize how fragile life is. I have also come to realize that that day on the river is a great metaphor for my life and my relationship with God. God has been a constant calming force in all of my overwhelming obstacles. He has always been there reminding me to be quiet and rest, to place my faith in him and know that he will provide refuge.

That story illustrates the experiential preceding the mental understanding. Similarly, running legend Alberto Salazar tells about his experience of having a heart attack, a fourteen-minute period during which he had no pulse. He shares his experience as a spiritual journey: "Everything that happens has a purpose. God has a plan for all of us. Sometimes we don't know what it is. We just have to keep searching. That's the whole thing about faith. You never know for certain what life will bring, or necessarily what God will want you do. It's a never-ending process. Sometimes we're going to muddle around and be confused. But there is always a reason."

Faith is a process. It usually begins in fear but it ends in joy and meaning. A number of years ago I took my child to the playground. Near us, by the climbing apparatus, was a father and his daughter, a girl of about five years. She had climbed up into the playhouse and was sitting in the door, her legs dangling over the edge. "Jump," called the father. "I'll catch you." "I'm afraid," she responded. "Don't worry," said her father. "I'm here." After much hesitation and with still some trepidation, she slid off the edge, falling into his arms. She jumped down from his arms, ran back up the stairs to the jumping area and gleefully jumped into her father's arms. She had faith he could and would catch her. Her grounded faith overcame her fear and led her to joy.

Faith is about relationship, expectancy, meaning, and risk; faith is about craziness, uncertainty, and adventure. From this chapter on what faith is and is not, the spotlight has been aimed at how faith is relational and meaningful, not absent of thinking, yet not dependent on thinking. Faith involves being in deep water with a grateful heart, before seeing the conclusion.

# CHAPTER THREE

# *Faith As Confluence*

When two or more rivers are becoming one, there must be turbulence at the connecting stage. After that intermingling and joining there is an eventual quieting. The experience of faith, too, deals with that turbulence as well as its subsequent resolution. The many components of the life of faith are often contradictory and messy, and our experience of them is messy. But the joining of disparate forces in faith reveals the paradox of such a life. In short, the life of faith is a life of confluence and paradox. Faith is simultaneously complex and simple.

Marcus Borg speaks of faith using the words "commitment, loyalty, and allegiance." Beyond mere concepts, these three attributes speak of relationship, for each implies an "other," someone to whom a commitment is made, loyalty is given, or allegiance is pledged. In each case, both persons in the relationship are affected. Whether the relationship is with your neighbor, your spouse, or God, all parties are potentially influenced. The persons placing faith and the persons receiving faith placed in them can be changed through the relationship, just as the rivers are changed during and after their confluence.

In this way, relationships are truly dynamic and constantly work to change experience. Just as the rivers during and after confluence change each other as well as the banks that contain them (and the new unified river), so in relationships the two—the one placing faith and the one receiving faith—work on each other, changing the other, augmenting the other. In the process, the worlds in which the two exist must change because of the relationship. The life of faith, when seen as confluence, necessarily becomes a causal agent, though with no certainty of what the effects will ultimately be. The process of confluence in faith is messy, turbulent, and metamorphic, but it does include times of smoothness, times when we see back on the experience and learn from it. Our faith increases, at least until the next confluence.

## *As our faith develops, so does our ability to construct meaning.*

Another metaphor might help us understand this time of smoothness and reflection. Imagine hiking a mountain and looking down from 1,000-foot elevation and then from 2,000 feet. The difference is striking. The higher perspective broadens the view, increasing holistic and comprehensive aspects of what is observed, yet details begin to get less pronounced. Ron Martoia says, "Stages of faith don't reflect as much hierarchy as they do our ability to hold increasingly greater amounts of complexity, ambiguity, and paradox in tension." As our faith develops, so does our ability to construct meaning.

Still, the development of faith does not mean that the tension and irony, the confluence, of life disappear. G. K. Chesterton reminds us of a recurring paradox within us—the relationship between reason and faith. We are often tempted to privilege reason over faith, but he reminds us that "Reason itself is a matter of faith. It is an act of faith to assert that our thoughts have any relation to reality at all." The confluence here has to do with knowledge or reason causing us to feel more self-sufficient and independent, thereby tempting us to reduce our dependence on faith. Chesterton, however, argues that even counting on our reasoning power is a demonstration of faith. You may have heard the saying, "reality is a collective hunch." As we move into the smoothness of the rivers joining, as we look down from higher elevations, we are humbled as we see the limitations of our reason even while we affirm its value. Faith and reason are reconciled in this perspective, and we open ourselves to further learning.

When we learn an added language as adults, or when learning anything at the entry level as adults, we find ourselves in a state of humility and must create an openness to absorb. Both of these conditions describe a reality of tumult and disturbance. When learning a language, we cannot fight its grammar and vocabulary, for we cannot change it to be how we want it to be, to conform to our favorite language. In experiencing the second language we actually learn more about our initial language in the act of juxtaposing the two languages.

Just as humbling, often, is the common human conundrum of contemplating our relationship with the Infinite. Whatever we call the Infinite—God, Being, the Other, etc.—when we contemplate our relationship to it, we are nonetheless aware of the limits of reason. Thrown back on the mystery of what we cannot fully grasp, we might be devastated, we might despair, but we certainly find ourselves in the turbulence of intellectual, experiential confluence. James E. Loder notes this in a specifically Christian context: "... faith is the transparency in which the eternal and the existential constitute a bipolar-relational unity which comes into being for the individual only after reason comes face to face with the paradox of the God-man—that is, after reason finds something it cannot think, and it declares the paradox 'absurd.'" That "bipolar-relational unity" is the calm after the rivers join, the view from 2,000 feet. But it comes not despite the tension between faith and reason but because of their messy interaction as we humbly stand in the mystery of the Infinite.

Terms like "certainty," "control," "doubt," and "faith" all thrown together can produce uneasiness. There are parts of life for which we need certainty. For that matter there are elements of life that are certain, like gravity. In many situations control is necessary in order to be successful. When riding a bicycle, besides balance, we "certainly" need control. We need to be relatively confident. Simultaneously we might have doubts about our confidence. And on and on the soliloquy continues, most of us having such a discussion in our brain throughout the day.

Speaking to these cognitive, paradoxical elements, Oswald Chambers declares, "Certainty is the mark of the common-sense life: gracious uncertainty is the mark of the spiritual life. To be certain of God means that we are uncertain in all our ways, we do not know what a day may bring forth. This is generally said with a sigh of sadness; it should be rather an expression of breathless expectation. We are uncertain of the next step, but we are certain of God. Immediately we abandon to God, and do the duty that lies nearest, He packs our life with surprises all the time." Gracious uncertainty. Breathless expectation. Surprises. These are indeed what we experience in the confluences of life.

## *If doubts and uncertainty exist, then faith is needed.*

❖

Faith is messy. Faith simultaneously interacts with knowledge, doubt, certainty, uncertainty, logic, and practicality, to name a few. If doubts and uncertainty exist, then faith is needed. If doubts do not exist, we have no need for faith, for knowledge overcomes the need for faith. Yet while certainty and knowledge exist in some, even many, situations, we have seen that total certainty and total knowledge are not possible. And so we will continue to encounter uncertainty, doubt, and finitude. As Philip Yancey notes, "Doubt always coexists with faith, for in the presence of certainty who would need faith at all?" Perhaps it is safe to say that there cannot be certainty, but there can certainly be meaning. If we strive toward certainty and miss meaning, the question posed could be, of what use? The wisdom in this notion is to build our world toward meaning (faith), not certainty.

Mixtures of the desire to control along with other ego matters are related to the "faith is messy" syndrome. Theoretical physicist Leonard Susskind says, "The first thing that physicists had to free themselves of—the thing that Einstein held so dear—was the notion that the laws of nature are deterministic. Determinism means that the future can be predicted if enough is known about the present." But can we ever know enough and can we be certain we know sufficiently? While we can think that if we can control knowledge, we can also have control, such control can backfire. Eric Barnhill, as a classical pianist, used to approach music-making as something to dominate, to control muscularly. Eric Liu, however, observed the problematics of that approach: "And the control he exercised became so overpowering, it so overcompensated for the tics and fidgets and the sheer speed of everything threatening to escape his body, that he played as if he and the piano alike were crammed into a tiny box." This overcontrol, a sign of anxiety, also compounded the anxiety.

A while ago, I took my racquet to the racquetball shop to be restrung. The owner asked me, "Do you want it strung for control or power?" I don't think I had ever thought about that choice before, and for the first time I expressed a new insight. "For control," I said. Before that I had thought that power was control. With the human body, pure power without flexibility eventually takes its toll, and a person is physically almost worthless. In my own playing of the marimba, I am attempting to play from my mind, not my muscles. It's a strange, seemingly illogical approach, but it's more life-giving to my body and to the music. Like scientists needing to deal with the unpredictability within quantum mechanics, having to accept random, uncontrollable elements as realistic may not be desired, but it is essential. We want control. The real question is, what is control?

Gregory Bateson noted the same situation within the social sciences: "Let me then conclude with a warning that we social scientists would do well to hold back our eagerness to control that world which we so imperfectly understand. The fact of our imperfect understanding should not be allowed to feed our anxiety and so increase the need to control. Rather, our studies could be inspired by a more ancient, but today less honored, motive: a curiosity about the world of which we are part. The rewards of such work are not power but beauty." Applied to athleticism, form and control subsume power, not the other way around. Pure power without the control coming through beautiful form and style brings about less accuracy and probable injury.

In some respects, the opposite of control is dependence. That term has various manifestations that give us some insights into the progression of faith and relationship. We noted earlier that out of the messiness and turmoil of experience we learn how limited we are. The result of that insight is humility—we acknowledge how ignorant or weak or incapable we are. That humility leads us to dependence. The progression after that point is generally the following: dependence, independence, and finally interdependence. Let's illustrate that paradigm using basketball. If you are not a very good player (perhaps you just learned the game, or maybe you are not very athletic and coordinated), once you get the ball you get it to a stronger player, almost immediately. With such fear and anxiety your best control is in the hands of a better player. That's dependence. As you improve as a player, you gain confidence in your own ability and take control of the ball more and more. In fact, you become a "ball hog" when you imagine yourself as better than anyone else on the team. That's independence, perhaps to the extreme. Finally, however, you learn that important lesson: basketball is a team sport, not an individual sport. You balance your choice to take the shot yourself and your choice to pass to a player who has a better chance of making the shot. You do that for the good of the team. That is interdependence.

In the life of faith, we often find that same progression. Most of us start from the status of dependence, recognizing the overwhelming superiority of the Other. But at some point, either after dependence or even before it, independence takes over when we begin to think about ourselves as superior even to the Other. We assume we can control from our position of power. But that is misperceiving reality. Donald McCullough talks about that dynamic from a theological perspective:

> Much of what drives us, as the first chapters of Genesis teach, is a desire to take God's place, an arrogant striving to seize control, to rise above the limitations of our humanity. The Bible calls this sin. Contrary to what you might have been told, God's preferred way of dealing with this problem is not to blast sinners into the fires of hell but to lift them into the joys of new life. To accomplish this, God chose to do something so remarkable, so utterly unthinkable, you'd have to be God

to come up with it: in Jesus Christ, God canceled our arrogance with a supreme act of humility. Whereas we have been doing our best to become like God, God chose to become human; whereas we have been reaching upward, God chose to bend downward; whereas we have been fighting against all limitations, God chose the most severe limitation; whereas we have been striving for self-fulfillment, God chose self-emptying; whereas we have been running for dear life, God chose death.

The irony here is that through humility and self-emptying God accomplishes interdependence as God works with us to develop us spiritually. That is the paradox of death producing life.

The Gospel of Matthew reports that Joseph was betrothed to Mary, who at the time was pregnant with a child from the Holy Spirit. Here was a supreme confluence of the divine and the human, of the infinite and the finite. How must Joseph have felt as he found himself in a situation beyond his imagining, and in some ways beyond his control? What would his attitude have been—anger? resentment? fear? confusion? What choices did he imagine when he was called to marry Mary, his beloved? Here actually was the realization of the paradigm of dependence, for finally Joseph, as well as Mary, experienced interdependence in relationship to God. We cannot reach God via the route of wisdom and reason, but we can move toward God in relationship by the response of faith in that which is and has been done for us. Faith is a letting go and surrendering. But in that surrendering is also a joining.

To illustrate this conflict of control with faith, I share a vignette from a medical doctor who often volunteers in third-world countries. In extremely constricted conditions he does surgeries and delivers babies. From one of his emails: "I started my time here being reminded that I was not in control, and I am finishing my time here being branded with the fact that I am not in control. But how I wish I would have taken control!" Then he closes his email saying, "Lord, for me tonight, please make my faith strong, strong enough to accept." His intermix of control with faith and then using the word "accept" reveals the challenge of living within a context where faith and control must coexist. Most of us would take certainty any day, yet the life we live requires faith.

Phrases such as "leaning in" and "letting go" move toward describing acts of faith. Some will not find these to be preferred or popular notions. Some prefer the existential angst of Jean-Paul Sartre and Albert Camus, who found the world to be without meaning. The fascinating paradox, however, is that such a response presupposes the understanding of a better possibility. Says Terry Eagleton, "Angst is just the flip side of faith." Our ability to think and imagine the way the world could be or the way we would like it to be presses hard against letting go. As Kathleen Norris reminds us, "Faith, of course, is not readily understandable, which makes it suspect among people who have been educated to value ideas insofar as they are comprehensible, quantifiable, consistent." She continues by pointing out that faith is less about ideology and more about experience, that humans will show a strong faith in something without proof or evidence. We all, for example, assume—that is, have faith—that the sun will rise tomorrow morning, or that the plane we are riding in will not crash.

Another paradox is that in order to let go, one must first have control—you can't give up what you don't have. And yet, that paradox is itself paradoxical, for in the process of relinquishing we find that we have been deceived by appearances. What appears to be chaos and disorder to us, to our rational minds, finally reveals itself as symmetry, order, and beauty. The mathematical study of fractals demonstrates that even the most random and chaotic structure finally displays itself in orderly mathematical equations. It is a matter of perspective.

We find that in the meaning-making of faith, the reality is not of our construction but is grounded in God, in Spirit. Whether we are on the bus or not is in some ways irrelevant; the point is God is driving the bus, and it is God's bus, not ours. How spiritual we feel or how dutifully we attempt to be spiritually disciplined does not determine truth. The Good News is about God's actions, not ours. Reality is far beyond our experiences. Reality is what produces and gives meaning to our experiences.

I have found freedom to be the surprising consequence of faith. Faith frees me to explore my thinking and to ask questions. Within the world of faith I am not bound to find certainty or to determine reality; my motivation is not to "find" faith or to decipher where to apply faith but rather to search and discover wherever my mind and heart lead me. To choose faith courageously is not to build a wall that excludes certain doubts and fears and questions. What I create is a foundation that supports me in my process of discovery as I welcome every inquiry, any question, all doubts. With faith in God and God's rules I can enjoy the pursuit of discovery. Susan K. Williams Smith aptly titles her book, *Crazy Faith*: "Faith is knowing the One in whom you trust, and moving and acting in a way that says you know. There is an assurance that what one knows will come to be. One doesn't know how it will come to be. One just knows that it will be. That knowledge also inspires one to work toward what is 'seen.' Faith is not sitting and waiting. It is moving toward the unseen; it is working and planning for what you see and know."

Faith can be simple or complex; in some respects it depends on the heuristic makeup and needs of the individual. Some persons need complex, thorough, scholarly, erudite explanations and evidences as a foundation for acting in faith. Their faith is no less real and no more valuable than the faith of those who are satisfied with not getting answers to questions they never asked. That simpler faith is similar to the type that Juan Williams and Quinton Dixie describe as the ". . . old-time religion of the slaves. Theirs was a faith that did not need to comprehend the poetics of the Hebrew language to know that God was true to his word when he delivered Daniel from a den of lions. Theirs was a faith that did not need to compare the Gospel of Matthew with that of Luke to get a more complete picture of the life of Jesus. All they needed to know was that he died for their sins and his blood cleansed them of all unrighteousness, and one day they would leave the troubles of this world for a better place. And in that place no one would ask their birth status as slave or free, whether they owned property or were sharecroppers, or whether they had enough education to write their names. No, all Jesus would say to them would be, 'Come unto me, all ye who are burdened and heavy laden and I will give you rest.'"

For some, however, this "simple" practice of faith is too unsophisticated, or perhaps too difficult. They see in that faith stance the need to acquiesce too easily to the challenge to have faith in the invisible, the spiritual. It's much easier to worship visible idols than Spirit God. We may think we know because of what we see, yet there is so much in life that is not seen. The ability to imagine the potential in anything is an act of faith. Through the use of imagination C.S. Lewis penned, "And that is precisely what Christianity is about. This world is a great sculptor's shop. We are the statues and there is a rumour going around the shop that some of us are some day going to come to life."

I teach a humanities course titled "Faith, Living, and Learning," a required upper-division college course. It serves as a time-out from knowledge-driven classes. It is not meant to challenge the faith of students, but it is certainly an opportunity for students to explore their faith, to see if it is truly their faith or simply an adopted faith. The three words—faith, living, and learning—can represent spirit, body, and mind. In any application this suggests an outstanding confluence. I believe that as students enter the first class they assume each of the three aspects to be separate; several weeks into the course, however, they discover how unified faith, living, and learning are.

Here is an exit reflection from one of the students in that course, one that might represent many: "My views on faith, living, and learning have been challenged because I was really expecting something totally different from this course. I thought that it would be something very much geared towards faith. In my mind going in I thought we were going to tackle such things as how we came to know the Lord and the journeys in getting there. Along the way I began to realize what faith, living, and learning were all about. I began to see that not only were we talking about faith but talking about living and its challenges and faith and its challenges and how we learn through our fun and disciplined faith."

What you are about to read might leave you wondering, yet by expressing faith within mystery, Annie Dillard's words express confluence. "Faith would be that God is self-limited utterly by his creation—a contraction of the scope of his will; that he bound himself to time and its hazards and haps as a man would lash himself to a tree for love. That God's works are as good as we make them. That God is helpless, our baby to bear, self-abandoned on the doorstep of time, wondered at by cattle and oxen . . . Faith would be, in short, that God has any willful connection with time whatsoever, and with us. For I know it as given that whatever he touches has meaning, if only in his mysterious terms, the which I readily grant. The question is, then, whether God touches anything. Is anything firm, or is time on the loose?"

*Part Two*
# Relationships and Improvisation

# CHAPTER FOUR

# *My Relational Improvisation Journey*

Beginning at age three I listened to music by the hour. I could not get enough. The medium was the radio, and I would tune it to the Los Angeles classical station, soaking it in passionately. Captivated by how compositions were organized, the textures of sound, and the pure beauty to my ear, I was hooked. Naturally I wanted to do it myself. With "Piano Parade" being a favorite program, I was particularly drawn to the piano. Without any instrument in our home, I made it clear to my parents that I would like a piano and a teacher. In the 1940s piano teachers were not inclined to teaching small hands, so rejection after rejection, until my parents found a teacher who said she taught both marimba and piano. Her suggestion was to introduce me to music and the keyboard via the marimba, a $25 fold up model. I was six and she said that when I was eight I could begin piano.

Apparently the lessons and learning went very well. A year later, due to such rapid growth playing the marimba, my parents purchased a four-octave instrument, a large commitment of physical space. It was housed in the living room, obviously quite a sacrifice. When I was eight I began piano, as per plan, while continuing marimba. The living room now had two large instruments commanding space. What parents! Two years later I added trumpet to my regimen. By the time I was ten, my morning practice schedule was set: 6:00 marimba, 6:30 piano, 7:00 trumpet, 7:30 breakfast. This allowed freedom in the afternoon for homework, playing outside, and exploring sound by fooling around at the piano. An early morning person by nature and having a penchant for discipline, I was making certain each week that my lessons were prepared just as the written assignment stipulated.

After one of my piano lessons I asked my teacher if I could share a short sample of sounds I had made up. Shock of shocks, her response was something to the effect that even doing this experimenting at the piano was a waste of time. Apparently the philosophy at that time was simply to read and play music of accepted composers. Learning the repertoire was the end-all. For me, this did not compute. I wasn't against this approach, but also I didn't feel limited to it, for there was a drive deep within myself to explore and "play around with sounds." I perceived life in both interpreting and improvising music.

The ultimate message I heard was the difference between what was considered worthy music and pointless music. It led me to think that music of value was already composed, and my role was to memorize it, not wasting my time adding my voice to tradition. Emotionally I found the rejection discouraging and isolating. Although I could play the stuff I was making up for family and friends, I really wanted to share this with my teacher. Because she refused to listen, the upshot in my mind was that play and freedom were devalued. My question became, why couldn't she have a high regard for the great composers *and* an openness to exploration? After all, didn't the established composers explore as a way to find out what they really wanted to write?

Believing that I didn't need to privilege one genre over another, I believed that both classical and popular forms of music could be held in high esteem. When I was in junior high school playing trumpet in the marching band, and still practicing and performing marimba and piano, I was also listening to recordings of big band jazz. Until that time I had been listening solely to classical music. Now I was also loving the output of Harry James and Les Elgar. Another sound I would listen to repeatedly was a popular trumpet tune, "Cherry Pink and Apple Blossom White," played by Raphael Mendez. It contained a glissando that wowed me, descending then returning on the melody. It was all about sound and emotional response. After I practiced my lesson for trumpet, I would try to mimic that piece by depressing the valves only slightly for the glissando effect. Fun and freedom.

Music meant listening, practicing, and exploring. I was equally devoted whether I was reading music or making it up. I began to realize that for many people the visual and aural approaches were viewed as distinct and hierarchical. For some persons, making music through reading was superior; for others, playing by ear was better. It became an outlook of right or wrong, but I just could not understand how right or wrong applied to music.

Listening to classical music *and* jazz music as a kid was natural for me, an enjoyment, an engagement with sound aesthetically. I was a listener and a player. It was musical expression that I received and produced and with which I tinkered. In my state of mind there was not a criterion of what's hip and not hip. There was simply my personal proclivity toward listening closely to music and finding a subsequent joy, whether it was classical or jazz.

During the 1940s and 1950s, jazz was experiencing mixed response. Many considered jazz to be overly complex and irritating and believed it had serious behavioral ramifications. In *The Anthropology of Music* Alan P. Merriam portrays the association of jazz with the ills of society: "It is not surprising that, given its supposed reversion to barbarism, jazz was also attacked as an anti-Christian symbol." This cultural moral opposition to jazz began to filter down to me. People began using the terms "legitimate" and "illegitimate" in discussing musical styles, and I felt uncomfortable when prompted to choose between the two.

By the time I began college in 1960, I loved listening to a variety of music. I could be captivated by Beethoven's *Fifth Symphony* one moment and then be emotionally overwhelmed by the rhythms and sounds of Dave Brubeck's *Take Five*. If a musical selection was high quality with a commensurate performance, I was good to go. Then one evening I was driving on the freeway when I heard the most beautiful and sweet trumpet piece on the radio. I needed to know who was playing with such a soulful sound. I was introduced to the world of Miles Davis. I began listening to him very intentionally, and soon included many of his cohorts.

I was mesmerized by the freedom of sound and endless ideas that emanated through his jazz expression.

The freedom I found in Miles Davis didn't fully work its way into my life, for I still found that the society around me tried to define me, to put me into categories, to place moral categories on my choices, tastes, and behaviors. Like any young person, I was still trying to define myself through a process of experimentation and discovery. I knew, for example, that if I told people I listened to Bach, Beethoven, and Brahms, they would consider me sophisticated. And the pressure existed to listen to those types of composers because I was told they were good, and if I listened to them I would be among the elite and the acceptable. Not so if I enjoyed lesser-known composers such as Hummel or "illegitimate" artists like Brubeck.

Without the culture telling me that I was fine or foolish, I was free to claim a personal response to what I was hearing. As the vibrancy of *Take Five* danced its way into my emotions and the soulful sound of Miles penetrated my being, all I knew was that I felt alive. These representative expressions were pushing my appreciation for improvisation. By finding a relatively free improvisational art form in jazz to stand alongside a more fixed compositional art form of classical music, my exuberance for listening and performing music was stretching speedily.

When I was pursuing a master's degree in percussion I was immersed in a world that included symphonic literature along with rock, Latin, and jazz styles. By definition percussion includes instruments that are struck, shaken, or scratched. The gamut is wide, from timpani used in orchestras with highly controlled literature to drum set used in popular idioms. My daily practice schedule included all sorts of styles and instruments. My teacher knew that I thrived on my classical underpinnings, but he could see in me the thirst for this other art form, jazz. One day he flat out asked, "Do you want to play jazz or not?" With those childhood impressions of jazz as wayward, I hesitatingly yet excitedly responded, "Yes!" I was twenty-eight, and it took guts to turn the corner and go for it. I knew I had the freedom to say no or yes, but by responding in the positive I knew I was committing. I now had a new responsibility, to add another language to my music-making. I had made a significant decision—to augment my life with the hard work of learning a new artistic expression called jazz improvisation.

Stepping officially into jazz as an active learning process meant a major shift into a very different arena of music. In classical styles I was confident as a professional artist. In jazz styles it took months and actually years of immersion and playing time to begin to sound like a jazz musician. In the classical realm I was taught how to read music and interpret it expressively. It was drilled into me and I practiced and demonstrated my skills publicly. The one-on-one instruction and coaching led me confidently into how I was to perform the music. Having experienced a cognitive approach to learning for twenty-eight years, I was now finding that jazz worked differently. You get experience by "sitting in" and trying your "chops" in live situations, not necessarily getting to polish a piece and then performing. You often find yourself playing with others for the first time, many of whom may be strangers who are virtually putting you to the test. Such a performance is rather risky and certainly "in the moment." It's finding out what's going to happen as it happens, quite unlike the classical mode.

So here I was ready to learn this art form of jazz, which is centrally about improvisation, but I also realized that I was not going to get clear directives from teachers showing me how to go about it. In fact, the rudest awakening occurred when I discovered that simply sprucing up a melody and feeling that I was improvising was farcical. Finding out that whatever type of varying the melody had to be done within "time" was an extreme shock to me. This alone demonstrated how uninformed I was about this improvisational art form. Whereas I had thought I could dink around with the melody, secondarily consider harmonic support, and at the bottom of the hierarchical heap take rhythm into the mix, I was now realizing that more than anything else I was to honor time and rhythm, as well as harmony within time; then, as I was able, I could deal with melody. What a jolt! Heretofore, I had thought all I had to do was knock 'em dead with a gorgeous melody. Time for a new mindset.

47

## *. . . meaning occurs as responsible freedom is applied within established constraints.*

Jazz pianist Randy Halberstadt says, "A young jazz musician often struggles to reconcile the opposing concepts of freedom and discipline in jazz. He will convince himself that he's exercising his freedom when he's really just being undisciplined. Watch out for this trap." I was shocked by my ignorance. I apparently thought that I was to engage freedom. What I did not understand was that improvisation is based on the "given," the structure, the essence upon which you exercise freedom. I was realizing that meaning occurs as responsible freedom is applied within established constraints.

Learning that improvisation was not simply changing the melody was radically eye-opening. This turned my former understanding of musical priorities upside down. I now believed the prioritized order of rhythm, harmony, and melody was a critical guideline to be used in improvisation. This supremacy of rhythm carried over into how I interpreted classical music. What I learned through the lens of jazz affected all of my music-making, and it spilled into how I saw organizations, family systems, and virtually all of life. For example, I had seen that often when a new manager or supervisor came into an office and immediately set about making changes without listening to the workers or trying to learn how things had been working, efficiency dropped and morale sagged. Now, seeing the situation through my new understanding of jazz, I realized that the manager (the melody) had usurped priority over rhythm (the structure and history of the department) and the harmony (the workers). No wonder there was a problem. Rhythm and harmony hold amazing power and must be reckoned with.

At this point in my development I wanted more formal guidelines to help instruct me. What I didn't realize was that I was entering the field of jazz education when it was just in its infancy. Nowadays it's quite sophisticated—there are textbooks galore and degree programs all the way up to the doctoral level. Remember that into the 1960s jazz was frowned upon by the dominant academic culture, and the music curriculum focused on classical music almost exclusively. In 1970 in Chicago the opportunities for jazz study were limited. There was one teacher that I learned of and one jazz instruction book available. And while most veteran jazzers would say to me, "just listen a lot and practice a lot," I still didn't know how to practice intelligently. I needed some type of bridge from the classical tradition to the jazz domain. What I wanted actually didn't exist at that time. I wanted a teacher who, like my classically-oriented past teachers, would lead me step-by-step into the world of jazz. That kind of coach/teacher just wasn't available. At that point I was dealing with two sources of conflict—how to learn jazz myself and how to find a teacher who could transition me from the classical mindset to the jazz approach.

Now having earned my master's degree, I was at a crossroad. I was eager to be employed and willing to go anywhere in the United States when, among some other options, a close friend from high school days, Randy Roth, gave me a distinct challenge. He knew of my newly-acquired improvisational fascination. He knew of my personal, spiritual faith. By implication he tied improvisation and faith together in planting an idea. He suggested that in faith Barb, one-year-old Matt, and I could move from Chicago to Portland, improvising a lifestyle to see what would happen. Randy's milking the improvisational concept to the extreme actually hooked me. My mind construed this as so preposterous that it became a vision we could live into. Trailer behind car, Barb and I placed Matt in his car seat and away we traveled west. I had such a feeling of total freedom as I was driving. The sense of adventure was beyond description. This truly was a juncture in our life, geographically and improvisationally. This was my initial seed of comprehending the confluence of faith and improvisation.

After arriving in Portland I began teaching privately. I found my-self playing piano, marimba, and vibes in any and many practice/garage bands, sometimes playing improvisationally in public. As in Chicago, it was difficult finding persons who knew how to steer a fledgling jazzer through the maze to learn how to improvise. Eventually I found a price-less teacher in Jerome Gray. His genius as a jazz pedagogue became my model. I learned both a path for my own development and a step-by-step approach for teaching others. These experiences ultimately energized my doctoral journey with its culminating dissertation's title saying it all: *An Integrated and Experiential Approach for Teaching Improvisation.*

I had been raised in a rather orderly fashion, beginning college as a Business Administration major, planning toward being an accountant, and moving through a potpourri of experiences until I eventually be-came a jazz musician enthralled with improvisation; I was now living in a world far removed from my beginnings as I embraced jazz, balanc-ing my otherwise methodical nature. Some persons fear this improvisa-tional mode. Others crave it. One of the finest jazz pianists I know, Randy Porter, said about improvisation, "I like surprises, things that you can't control, the mystery and the unknown that transcend preparation." It is about risk, adventure and spontaneity. Such a description may sound wonderfully attractive to some and seriously repulsive to others. For me, exploring the freedom within improvisation was and is worth every bit of energy I apply.

There are countless expressions of freedom beyond musical and lifestyle improvisational stories. In fact, I believe we are all born with the ability to improvise. David, of Old Testament fame, wrote poetry on beautiful hills and during lonely nights while tending his sheep. David used his role as shepherd to connect with his Maker. One of his Psalms begins, "The Lord is my shepherd." And from that metaphor David built a poem. This is David improvising. You and I can improvise from our vo-cation concerning our relationship with someone. Our imagination can choose an expressive way to use our freedom. I believe that we have both methodical and carefree sides and that we appreciate both the predict-able and the unexpected elements. Here is the poem that comes out of David's improvisation while shepherding, Psalm 23:

The Lord is my shepherd;
I have all that I need.
He lets me rest in green meadows;
he leads me beside peaceful streams.
He renews my strength.
He guides me along right paths,
bringing honor to his name.
Even when I walk
through the darkest valley,
I will not be afraid,
for you are close beside me.
Your rod and your staff
protect and comfort me.
You prepare a feast for me
in the presence of my enemies.
You honor me by anointing my head with oil.
My cup overflows with blessings.
Surely your goodness and unfailing love will pursue me
all the days of my life,
and I will live in the house of the Lord forever.

To live by following the script alone is to live partially. It's like learning to write letters of the alphabet, even words, and then being limited to copying sentences written by others, never being able to create poetry or describe a sunset in writing. Jazz, both as a musical form but even more as a way of liv-ing, is all about being both free and responsible, about a dynamic creativity. Colleen Shaddox says, "In jazz, anybody can sit in. It's dogma-free, which al-lows the music to take more than its share of detours. This forces you to have faith. Faith that if you keep moving forward, you'll get there."

## *Jazz improvisation functions to correct those destructive attitudes. I can accept being less than perfect.*

By diving into the jazz world I have noticed how its processes can affect every domain of life. With a personality prone to perfectionism, I learn from the jazz idiom other ways to view life. If, as I am improvising, I am thinking of controlling my output, pushing for perfection, I can easily become self-critical, scolding myself for what I have done. Jazz improvisation functions to correct those destructive attitudes. I can accept being less than perfect.

Let me use an anecdote from my own experience to illustrate this relationship between the freedom of improvisation and the bondage of perfectionism. I was invited by stellar players to be part of their ensemble. Our gigs had jazz aficionados as the core of the audience. These are listeners whose ears easily distinguish the formulaic from artful creativity, a creativity that can come only from the vulnerability of letting go and truly improvising. I knew they expected mature soloing. These factors—the sophistication of the audience and the fact that the other band members were thoroughly devoted to their instruments and jazz itself—caused me to think myself into a frenzy. I feared failure and rejection. For a few months I was overwrought thinking myself unworthy; I knew that I couldn't cut it. I lacked inner confidence. On the other hand, my mind would reason that they invited me into their group. Surely if they had trust in me, why shouldn't I? Still, I struggled internally. It was agonizing having to deal with such a phenomenal opportunity. I could not reasonably decline their offer, but I also had to live with my fear and anxiety daily.

At last, a moment of release came. After sharing my dilemma with a friend, and after he had listened to my ranting for several minutes, he simply said, "It sounds like you fear appearing a fool." I understood, and accepted, the truth of his statement, and suddenly I gained inner freedom. I thought to myself that if I really lived into such fear wholeheartedly, I would not even get out of bed in the morning to take chances to appear a fool. Why would any of us take the risk to be criticized? I know I cannot control others and their responses to me. All of us, once we think about this seriously, realize that we must let go and be. I must ask myself what I want to do and move in that direction. In my case I wanted to play jazz, improvise, and play with skilled musicians. Once I accepted myself and put in my best effort with lots of preparation, my music-making took on a sense of joy. Instead of expending needless energy on worrying, I let go of my fear and applied positive energy.

Mine is not a singular story, however. Each of us is faced with this tension between the formulaic and the improvisational, the known and the unknown, the expected and the explorative. By choosing the "jazz" option, whether always or just often, we can get a sense of freedom and the joy it brings.

# CHAPTER FIVE

# *What Improvisation Is and Is Not*

*. . . improvisation is fully rational, and reasonable, as well as intuitive . . .*

My own life journey, with its mixture of bondage and freedom, was becoming a lifestyle of joyous preferences, and with that change I began to think even more seriously about what the word "improvisation" entails and what value it might have. If we think about improvisation as something irrational or as mere random choice, we might think it useless or frivolous. But the truth is that as humans we improvise continually, relying on it to give us pleasure as well as overcome challenges daily. In fact, improvisation is fully rational, and reasonable, as well as intuitive, and thus can be developed and enhanced.

The following story illustrates the intersection of the rational and intuitive modes. One evening I was with two friends, one a musician, one not. Howie, the musician, and I had been improvising on some jazz tunes and Jim, the non-musician, had been listening. Jim had heard us improvise on tunes before, but on this occasion he wanted to talk about improvisation, so Jim asked us to improvise freely, not based on any pre-determined structure (in this case, the lead sheets we had had in front of us). We improvised freely and joyously. After we finished, Jim was excited and surprised—he said that he had heard our individual voices when we had been playing the structured tunes, but now, in the freeplay, he heard those very same personalities. That an untrained ear could detect the "person" somewhat surprised me, not having attempted this experiment before. I learned that in both cases logic and intuition functioned to communicate the personality of the musician. Because we cannot get away from ourselves, we can expect our reason and our intuition will work together to reveal our particular personalities.

Think about doodling or shooting baskets in the driveway. Both of these activities represent an intersection of skill and spontaneity; both are kinds of play in which there is no real competition and few if any rules. In both we enter the activity with no expectations of having a winner; the only expected outcome is joy or fun for the participants. Daniel J. Wiener claims that "... improv does not constitute an escape from reality so much as permission to create and explore new realities, to experience imagined truth as present truth. Improvising is a way of returning to the immediacy of childhood play—fortunately, most of us remember that play was enormously satisfying, even though we have lost our easy access to it." That is the essence of play as well as the essence of improvisation.

When lost in play, we are lost in time. "In the moment" itself is an expression of freedom, a release from clock consciousness. This enviable childhood state brings happiness and well-being because in being released from temporality we are free from some of the limitations common to the human condition. When we can focus on our playing outside of time, we have no concern about obligations, responsibilities, or competing matters. On the other hand, the demands and routines of adulthood can sap the original zest and spontaneity from us. To move into play helps us return to the timeless world of childhood and regain its joy. This practice as an active attitude toward life is described by Jon Kabat-Zinn: "Mindfulness means paying attention in a particular way: on purpose, in the present moment, and nonjudgmentally. This kind of attention nurtures greater awareness, clarity, and acceptance of present-moment reality." Kabat-Zinn's description speaks to the essence of improvisation, where each player actively and intentionally listens to, and responds to, the world of the other.

As children we do not have trouble with the condition of our mind in its natural state, which is to accept disorder as richness. Such a jungle-like condition, so organic, adjusts readily to the unexpected. As we "mature," let's say, to fifteen years and older, we begin to have misgivings regarding disorder as we seek more knowledge and control. There are some adults, however, who are aware of their childlike freedom and can handle, even appreciate, the risky elements, which they find life-giving.

Such an adult is soprano sax player extraordinaire Steve Lacy, for he can handle, even relish, the messiness of jazz. He states why he is greatly attracted to improvisation: "It is something to do with the 'edge.' Always being on the brink of the unknown and being prepared for the leap. And when you go on out there you have all your years of preparation and all your sensibilities and your prepared means but it is a leap into the unknown. If through that leap you find something then it has a value which I don't think can be found in any other way."

Lacy's statement refers to the combination of preparation and exploration. A child is being prepared by exploration, which is how we learn. In this connection consider how we were able to balance well enough to stand before taking our first steps, and all of this before learning cognitively about balance and the body. We learned to speak before we were informed what words to use and how to arrange them in sentences. As we became competent in language, in due time we were able to think or not think about what we were doing while doing it.

*. . . when the jazz is going well and there are no hesitations in the playing, when the players are totally in the moment, there is absence of thinking.*

When deeply involved in improvising, when the jazz is going well and there are no hesitations in the playing, when the players are totally in the moment, there is absence of thinking. This is paradoxical. For example, in jazz improvisation the soloist senses the direction of the music that is developing, and if he or she goes with it, then the player makes new sense and simultaneously adjusts to the new sense just being made. Both "with-it-ness" and "lostness" are simultaneously occurring. This requires concentration, an absorption, which allows the person to be changed by what he or she hears and feels.

With all this involvement of play, timelessness, and the unknown, it can be tempting to want to protest how all this is irrational and hence not worth serious consideration in the first place. But, while these child-like characteristics are essential, there's no getting around the fact that improvisation itself is rational. Great jazz improvisers, while sounding complex and convoluted, are indeed building solos exhibiting structure and logic. If you analyze the solo of a proficient jazzer, you will find that the better the improviser, the more she will use the same elements as the greatest composers. Subconsciously, a fine musician, either by composing on paper or on the spot, applies attention to order, mitigating the perception of sheer wildness. An uninitiated listener may think that the jazz musician is making up stuff out of thin air, which in a sense is always true in improvisation, but the skilled improviser is actually using years of practice in constructing a convincing solo. Those years of preparation enable the jazz improviser to demonstrate a highly disciplined art of theme and variation. It's not created out of nowhere, but rather it is birthed from somewhere. It's not about stumbling in the dark but the result of a great deal of training and experience. When improvisers feel they are running out of ideas, they need more preparation and practice. The point here is that improvisation is disciplined imagination.

The basis for the improvisation has to be so solid that the improviser, when in the process, is free not to think. It is very similar to language acquisition whereby you master a repertoire of phrases, then gradually you construct on-the-spot with decisions about how to sequence them. When you are in conversation with someone and you know what you want to communicate, you choose your words and sentence structures uncon-sciously (and consciously) in order to help the other person understand your idea and feel your emotion.

Stellar trumpeter Wynton Marsalis, born into a family of jazz creators, talks about listening to adult conversation as a kid and finding it hard to follow, but later, having more mature instincts, being able to get a sense of things. He transfers this concept to understanding music, an awareness level he did not have as a kid: "Then, one day, I could actually understand—not in my mind but in my heart. It came to me all of a sudden. What he was playing made perfect sense, actually super-sense. These musicians were telling stories. And these bittersweet stories unfolded in unpredictable ways. The musicians themselves were often surprised by their inventions. But they worked with the surprises the way a bull rider adjusts his weight and angles to stay onboard."

Just as the bull rider works with the movements of the bull in order to maintain stability, so the improviser commits to the "bull" of structure. When improvising, the musician sometimes encounters structures that seem difficult, even overwhelming or impossible. The challenge is to work within those structures, to move with the challenges in order to stay with the music. The "bull" is important to the ride. Without tight organization and stipulated boundaries, or in one word, "structure," improvisation can become meaningless. If a person dislikes or feels uncomfortable with the particular structure, the difficulty in improvising increases. There must be a set of constraints that guide the improvisation. A chess player has freedom because of the board with its squares and the player's knowledge of possible moves. The fixed element provides a basis for movement within it. A road map guides the journey but offers options that allow for flexibility. This speaks to the dialectical process of creativity, of the interaction of the fixed and the flexible. When the improviser is faithful to a set of guidelines, the result demonstrates a dynamic simultaneity embracing both the fixed and the flexible.

Jazz musicians usually use what is called a "chart," a sheet that gives them information about the piece: notes that give the melody, chords that give the harmony, and some indicators of rhythm. In jazz you depend on the chart. You have agreed to work within its imposed constraints. You are virtually conversing with the material, keeping the melody in mind, knowing where you are while deepening and making it more complex through the purposeful play of improvisation. This is creativity within constraints. The rules may be overt or covert; nevertheless they serve as guidelines that structure expectations and conventions. This is the dialectic of the determined and the undetermined or the known and the unknown. Responding to something solid allows not only freedom but also advantageous security.

MRI scans reveal that when persons are improvising there is increased activity in two areas of the brain—one dealing with decision-making and the other dealing with language. When we dream, the same thing happens. The inhibition switch goes off and the self-expression switch goes on; thus our dreams are varied, even colorful and wild. In creative thought and spontaneous activity, that large region of the brain involved in monitoring our own performance is shut down. I find it intriguing to realize that Duke Ellington as a composer considered himself more of a dreamer than a pianist. He penned his dreams into compositions.

*Jazz is a kind of story telling in which the musician, along with the audience, goes on a journey of discovery and exposition.*

Dreams don't necessarily follow the form of our waking reality, but they finally do make sense, as Freud reminds us. Jazz is a kind of story telling in which the musician, along with the audience, goes on a journey of discovery and exposition. To do that well, the musician must give in to those creative parts of the brain that the MRI had indicated. Improvisation is about saying "Yes," even though the tendency for many is to avoid danger and risk. If the energy is not flowing, then what takes place is negative, a blocking, a saying "No." While our protective behavior may well produce control, what's needed is a letting go, a following of a journey to an end that isn't known and with an outcome that is only discovered enroute.

Admittedly there are some misconceptions about improvisation. It may be thought of as random and chaotic, but it is actually an art governed by rules. It's not what sometimes it seems—totally arbitrary, free, and unstructured—except as it's free within structure. That creative freedom is at the heart of jazz, but rigidity, fixity, legalism, and dogmatism all imply control and incapacitate creativity. What is needed, of course, is a letting go.

When speaking about improvisation I prefer to avoid the phrases "faking it" or "winging it," for they suggest inadequate preparation, as if improvisation is inconsequential and frivolous. When improvisation is lacking in design and method and comes off as a completely ad hoc activity, it really is not improvisation at all but is something else, a pseudo-improvisation, unworthy of the term. Improvisation requires skill, devotion, preparation, training, commitment, depth, and complexity, all terms implying responsibility. Not aimless and without control, true improvisation describes one of the most rigorous human endeavors. Eric Liu distinguishes two words related to improvisation—extemporaneous and impromptu: "Extemporaneous is not to be confused with impromptu. In impromptu, it's just bang and you're off. In extemp, you are given the topic and time to prepare, albeit only minutes. Before you step onstage, you have to make a plan."

The word "improvisation" is derived from the Latin *im* (not), *pro* (before), and *visus* (see), something which has not been seen in advance, hence, unforeseen and unexpected. I find the word "unforeseen" as extremely accurate and helpful in grasping the feel for the word "improvisation." Being able to foresee something implies prearrangement, agreed upon beforehand. Sort of a done deal, it's just waiting to be realized. In contrast, what takes place as unforeseen involves the openness to go wherever it goes in the moment. It's unpremeditated, unpredictable, and unexpected, all suitably associated terms. Out of the process of improvisation something new and unforeseen emerges. The words "emerge," "emergent," and "emergency" swirl around improvisation, the result of an evolutionary process, or emergent evolution. An emergency situation unexpectedly arises. It then requires flexibility and versatility. There's a suddenness to it. Thus we see an element of improvisation in these emergings.

In the case of musical improvisation, the creativity occurs during the process of performance, denoting an open-endedness, allowing spontaneity. According to Daniel J. Wiener, "Spontaneity can be defined both as an ability to experience and express fully, without inhibition, and as an ability to respond externally to new situations in an immediate, creative, and appropriate manner. Yet spontaneity can also be thought of not so much as an ability as a state of being, the presence of the timeless present."

Improvisation, which is art, is to be distinguished from craft. By its very nature, craft has a particular and known end in mind. Improvisation has an unknown or unrealized end, one that is discovered only in the process of experimentation and sequential discovery. Craft, while often beautiful and pleasing, is usually formulaic and often is functional; art, improvisation, although it adheres to rules, is neither utilitarian nor formulaic. To learn a craft, the craftsman needs to replicate the master carefully; to develop art, the artist must experiment and discover. My friend Wayne tells the story of how he wanted to learn flower arranging so he could make what his friend Susie always brought forth—aesthetic creations. He joined several others in her class, positioned himself at the front so he could copy her step by step as she instructed while demonstrating. When the teaching-through-doing was complete, he looked at his arrangement and compared it to Susie's. They were notably different. His outcome just didn't make it. He didn't like it. He couldn't believe his eyes. He told Susie that he followed her every placement and did as she did, to which she said, "I didn't know what I was doing until I was done." In craft you know what you are doing; in art you don't know what you are doing. Within the doing it, you are finding out what you are doing—an act of faith.

In many respects, improvisation is much like children at play. They get together; they determine the roles and rules; they may even suggest a purpose (though it isn't necessary); and then away they go, with delight and abandon. As they play, they don't try to go back and fix a mistake, or if they want to make a change, that "correction" becomes part of the game. Their play doesn't focus on a certain product; rather, it is a creative process. If the play were structured—Little League or Youth Soccer, for example—things would be different, for there would be imposed rules, clear expectations of right and wrong, winners and losers. But the play is improvised, and perfection is not part of the game. Those involved in the play don't plan every step (they don't foresee) and they don't calculate. That is how improvisation is. Engaging the imagination to guide the action in an unplanned way, improvisation allows continual split-second adjustments, playful discoveries, joyful collaboration, and personal indeterminacy. Improvisation, like play, involves the whole being—the physical, intellectual, spiritual, and emotional; it entails all the characteristics of life.

To improvise includes the free and natural flow of intuitive processes. Once restraints and limitations are established, you're free to "let go," a key description of improvisation. Once the structure is agreed upon, such as children stipulating what roles they will play, then comes the appropriate surrender of conscious control. It's whatever comes out, no censoring. Instead of attempting to remove or resolve the tensions, you accept them, live them, work them, and play them. You are being spontaneous, interacting with the original material. Such unpredictability produces results that, because they are not fully controlled, may fall admittedly within a continuum somewhere between the serendipitous and the calamitous.

Of course, the play of improvisation is best experienced with others. Certainly it is possible to play alone—in dancing, in humming, in improvising—but it is more fun to share the process with others.

Whether it's jazz, theater, quilting, classroom teaching, basketball, or visual art expressions, the experience has significant social interactive aspects. In this kind of group improvisation, everyone participates and each has an important place in the experience. While certain individuals may be more prominent in their roles at times, the whole group provides a context for a "soloist" to emerge. Everyone responds to one another. Saxophone player Joshua Redman makes the same point when he speaks of "an approach of adventurousness, risk, spontaneity, immediacy, and honesty. It's improvisation, and not improvisation purely as one guy taking a solo but improvisation as a whole esthetic commitment. That I think is the heart and soul of jazz. That's the attitude, the spirit, and that's what's primary."

This kind of collaborative improvisation is not limited to music, of course. It can occur in other areas, such as cooking. Imagine two capable cooks in a kitchen. Each could produce an excellent meal alone, but here they are working together. As they combine their skills they are constantly shifting perspectives and constantly tinkering with ideas. In their interacting the cooks alternate leader and follower roles with the collective goal of inventing the future. They must push as a team to transcend tradition into the unknown. From her book *The Improvisational Cook*, Sally Schneider says: "One of the most exciting sources of inspiration is collaboration with another cook. You bring your mutual sensibilities to bear in a kind of spontaneous free association that starts with a simple conversation. Ideas build and spark each other, one dropped for a better refinement, another added, until gradually the concept for a dish emerges." In joint improvisation all involved view one another as equal participants, receive the influence of the other, recognize and welcome the diversity in the other, demonstrate mutual respect, practice childlike interaction, and are comfortable with the metaphor of "play."

Much the same can be said in other areas when we think about collaboration and improvisation among individuals. Basketball great Kareem Abdul-Jabbar writes this in his book *On the Shoulders of Giants: My Journey Through the Harlem Renaissance*:

Many people unfamiliar with jazz think the music is all about the solo riffs. A single player suddenly jumping to the front of the stage, the spotlight shining brightly on him, while he plays whatever jumble of notes that pop into his head. But really, jazz is just the opposite. True, there are magnificent solos, but those moments aren't the point of jazz, they are all part of the larger musical piece. Each person is playing as part of the team of musicians; they listen to each other and respond accordingly. When the time is right, one player will be featured, then another, and so on, depending upon the piece. Indeed there is improvisation, but always within a musical structure of a common goal.

Same with basketball. When you play basketball, everything is timing, just as with a song. You must be able to instantly react to the choices your teammates make. You must be able to coordinate your actions with your teammates and you must understand when you need to take over the action—when to solo—and when to back off. The timing of group activity is a major part of basketball, as it is with jazz. A team of basketball soloists, without the structure of a common goal, may get TV endorsements for pimple cream, but it doesn't win championships.

Successful improvisation requires rapport, interconnectedness, and the awareness of the others. Within that context spontaneity can occur. Abdul Jabbar continues, ". . . jazz has a unique combination of being explosive yet controlled, measured yet unpredictable."

Improvisational theatre adds to our understanding the notion that the audience is not an observer but a participant, for the actors respond not only to fellow actors but also to the members of the audience. Regardless of any prior rehearsal, when the play begins in front of the audience, a new, interactive character is introduced.

The potential magic that comes forth from improvisational theater can excite mystery even more than what we find in conventional theater. The mixture of virtuosity and spontaneity produces lines almost too good to have been improvised; the end is a mysterious amalgam of unpredictability, surprises, and sophisticated "play." Within this unknown factor come high adventure, suspense, and vulnerability that heighten our intrigue and provoke us to wonder how it will come out.

The play, collaboration, and vulnerability of improvisation carry with them the real possibility of "failure," of getting out of sync with the band, having the cake fall, or missing a layup. But that is more than a part of improvisation; it is also essential to it. The risk involved in facing a challenge necessitates the chance that all may not be well, and it is part of the excitement for all the participants to experience the unforeseen outcome. Too many see failure as a moral or psychological error, but rightly understood it is a step to freedom. The improviser needs to be free to fail in order to be free to succeed.

I had an adult piano student who had practiced a piece conscientiously, but her anxiety, her fear of making a mistake, kept her from playing it well. As she played, missing note after note, she became increasingly frustrated and impatient. Finally I said to her, "I have an idea. Play to fail." She looked at me in astonishment. She had been attempting *not* to fail; when told to fail, she was suddenly freed to play what she had prepared.

Traditional schooling often focuses on objective standards, on getting the answers right, on avoiding mistakes. Conventional education privileges the left hemisphere of the brain because it deals with objective facts that can be tested and verified. But neuroscience tells us that we operate initially from the right side, the center of experience and subjectivity. The implication for education is clear: if our strong suit is our natural curiosity and desire to learn, and not to be worried about correct responses and rewards for avoiding failure, then we need to change our methodology as well as our attitude.

As children we were ready to explore and experiment without being anxious about whether we were right or wrong. We wanted to play; we wanted the experiences. Subsequently we were ready to deal with our left hemisphere as we learned how to correct weaknesses. Both hemispheres of the brain need to be in action, in tandem, with an attitude toward process being significant. By focusing only on perfection and avoiding errors, we lose the freedom to be.

## *Improvisation by definition is an imperfect art.*

Of course we do not begin by trying to make mistakes, but countless stories remind us that we can learn by going about something the wrong way. Recognizing we are fallible, we can find freedom to fail. Improvisation does not have guarantees. Mistakes can be regarded as opportunities for positive thoughts, ideas, emotions and so forth. Improvisation by definition is an imperfect art. One of the temptations for a neophyte in jazz improvisation is to be afraid of playing a wrong note. Trying to avoid mistakes swings one into control mode, the antithesis of improvisation. If the player succeeds in avoiding all wrong notes, the solo is usually not great or exciting, for the energy went into prevention instead of expression. The confident player can somehow immediately turn a mistake into an exciting choice and use it to work on behalf of the music. When a person steps into improvisation, the given attitude must be acceptance of imperfection as well as excellence.

Alan Arkin is a well-known and respected actor. Yet even he was aware of how he continually faced the possibility of failure when he worked as an actor in Second City, Chicago's improvisational theatre company. He said of this experience,

> But most importantly, the thing that separated my experience at Second City from every other endeavor I've ever been connected with was that we were in an arena where we were allowed to experiment. To change. To grow. And not only that, we were . . . allowed

to fail. *Allowed to fail!* And audiences came to the theater knowing this was very likely to happen. They knew that part of every evening wasn't going to work. They came to Second City to see process unfold, and they knew that if one scene was terrible there was every possibility the next one would be memorable.

As I reflect on improvisation's many aspects and ramifications, I realize how many factors it involves: imperfection, risk, freedom within constraints, structure, disciplined imagination, "in the moment," the unexpected, spontaneity, listening, exploration, discovering, preparation, an interactive conversational element, and the sense of play. All of these contribute to the joy of improvisation, as the unforeseen becomes manifest.

# CHAPTER SIX

# *Improvisation As Confluence*

"There are two kinds of people in the world—those who start a sentence with 'There are two kinds of people in the world' and those who don't." In so much of life we are prone to separate people, experiences, things, and so on into categories, often two, and to make judgments based on those distinctions. Sometimes that is helpful, but more often it is not. We begin to think that if you are in one category you can't be in the other. We noted in the last chapter that indeed the brain is separated into two hemispheres—the left, with its facility in reason and objectivity, and the right, with its emphasis on the experiential and the subjective. We also noted that often, in education and in living out our individual lives, we can focus on one side to the detriment of the other. But, as we noted, both need to be nourished.

When we think about improvisation as a way of life more than as just being limited to jazz, we discover that both sides of the brain, the whole person, in fact, are needed in experiencing our world and ourselves to their fullest. When we think in terms of "There are two kinds of people in the world, those who improvise and those who don't," we deprive ourselves of freedom and meaning. Let me use an illustration to suggest how bringing the two sides of the brain together can start to produce wholeness.

A clarinet player in a professional orchestra on the east coast was attending a clarinet convention in St. Louis. He was able to stay with a friend in the area. On the first evening, his friend took him to a party, a gathering totally unrelated to music. The host, not a musician but clearly a lover of music, displayed musical instruments around the house as pieces of art. The visiting clarinetist was admiring the clarinet in the collection when the host noticed him looking at the instrument. "Do you play the clarinet?" the host inquired. "Well, actually I do," he responded. "I am in an orchestra back home." "My, that is wonderful!" exclaimed the host. "Won't you honor us by playing something for the guests? We would be so pleased." The clarinetist was about to agree, but he quickly realized that without a music stand and a printed score he had nothing to offer. He was unable to express anything meaningful with the instrument on which he was so proficient. At this moment the musician realized how one-sided he was. He could make music if he had the notes written in front of him, but could not play by ear or improvise. This revealed to him how lopsided (one could even say "lobesided") he was.

When the clarinetist returned home, he found a teacher who could help him improve his improvisational skills. That is, could develop the other side of his brain. As his improvisational skills improved, he became increasingly free, and whole. What a transformation! Although he was technically proficient, enough so to excel at auditions for a prominent orchestra, the clarinetist had been bound to the printed score. Until having this encounter at the party, he had not realized his restriction. Once he acquired the confidence to make music without the written score, he now had more freedom when interpreting and playing written music. Improvisation had enlarged his musical, and personal, experience.

Because music is sound, not sight, we would expect the natural order of learning to be sound before sight; yet many music students are taught sight before sound, to see notes before they play on the instrument. Why is this so? Perhaps it is because the visual is based on something written, something tangible and permanent, something that can be manipulated and controlled. Sound isn't like that. It is evanescent, fleeting, uncontrolled. The visual connects to the intellect, but the aural connects to the existential, the emotional. Iain McGilchrist expresses this in terms of the brain: "So the left hemisphere needs certainty and needs to be right. The right hemisphere makes it possible to hold several ambiguous possibilities in suspension together without premature closure on one outcome." Favoring sight over sound privileges control over experience.

The urge to control is probably natural, and it is also understandably defensive. In a 1924 periodical written for piano teachers, Will Earhart confirms this point in outrageous fashion: "I do not approve of 'jazz' because it represents, in its convulsive, twitching, hiccoughing rhythms, the abdication of control by the central nervous system—the brain. This 'letting ourselves go' is always a more or less enticing act. Formerly we indulged it in going on an alcoholic spree; but now we indulge it by going (through 'jazz') on a neural spree." For Earhart, and for many others, there is great fear and anxiety in losing control—whether through alcohol, drugs, or jazz—because to do so would be to relinquish one's essential humanity. Ironically, what is lost in this need to control is wholeness.

Notated music provides a greater sense of certainty and control. You can learn to decode the signs and translate them to an instrument; in improvisation the results are unpredictable and uncertain. The same holds true in life. We may choose simply to follow the rules, hoping to retain control and predictability, thereby achieving certainty; on the other hand, we may risk going beyond or outside the rules and live into the ambiguous and uncertain world of adventure and discovery. This latter approach relinquishes a degree of certainty and encourages us to act within a framework of faith.

When a person is limited to a single, usual, determined choice through this quest for certainty, life itself is limited. How easy it is to fall into routine in our daily choices—taking the same route to work, having the same breakfast, sitting in the same pew in church. But that habit can limit our experiences. I remember a serious-minded eighty-year-old at the health club. I noticed he used the same showerhead every morning. Out of sixteen options he used one and only that one, whether there were five others showering or no one else. One day someone else was showering at "his" favored spot, and the otherwise very friendly older gentleman glared at the guy who was using his showerhead. His compulsive habit was disrupted, and he felt helpless to shower until the other man got out of the way. Had he been free to use any of the other fifteen showerheads, his experience might have been very different. He could have seen the room from a new perspective and could have known a new sense of freedom.

Mt. Hood is a volcanic mountain that stands unobstructed by other high peaks. One can drive or hike around its flanks and observe its magnificence from different perspectives. By seeing the mountain from more than one perspective, the viewer can gain a more complete appreciation of its grandeur, just as the old man in the shower could have gotten a more complete experience. It might be simpler to be content with one view of Mt. Hood, and it would still be a magnificent mountain from a single perspective. If one chooses to be so self-limiting, however, one will miss the wholeness that can be achieved through synthesis. One would be deprived of something worthwhile and satisfying. This notion is eloquently expressed by James E. Loder: "Complementarity is the logical relation between two descriptions or sets of concepts applicable to a single phenomenon or object which, though mutually exclusive, are nevertheless both necessary for a comprehensive description of the phenomenon or object."

To see Mt. Hood from one perspective is static singularity. To move around it is a process of multiplicity. As you move around it you discover it, and only at the end can you construct the whole in your experience. Process is everything. I once got a call in the afternoon to be a substitute in a professional ensemble for that evening's jazz gig. I showed up with my vibraphone. Before one of the tunes, I asked the drummer for a general idea of how the tune was to be approached, the feel and groove, to which he replied, "I'll tell you after we play it." I felt out of control because I lacked certainty. What I should have realized was that I had to let go, to trust, to have faith in myself, my musicianship, and my ear. The experience and not the talking about it in advance held the key.

It reminded me of the difference between the tightrope walker talking about the experience and actually stepping out onto the rope. Isn't the only way to know about tightrope walking to actually walk on the tightrope? It is about discovery, learning by doing. In an article titled "Making Sense of Improvisation," Crossan and Sorrenti explain that "[o]ne route to experimental learning is through improvisation. Given the subconscious nature of intuition, action precedes understanding with improvisation. We act, and then make sense of it afterward." The same principle is applied to innovation stated by Keith Sawyer: "Innovation emerges from the bottom up, unpredictably and improvisationally, and it's often only after the innovation has occurred that everyone realizes what's happened. The paradox is that innovation can't be planned, it can't be predicted; it has to be allowed to emerge." These statements introduce the element of chronology, experiencing relationships between activities over time, so we can reflect on the past, as historians do.

We can trace the development of a style by noting its roots in the past. A student of history can observe how the structure of the previous period is constantly brought into question, eventually moving away from the familiar until something different emerges. We are formed by the past while we simultaneously create something new. In pointing out the dependence of the present on the past, I'm highlighting the relational or dialectic nature of history. In the improvisational process the engagement of the known and the unknown, the semi-spontaneous and the spontaneous, goes forward toward an organically cultivated cohesion. History, too, plays a role in improvisation, as each participant brings a history and each element being engaged has its history. Interaction is not merely between persons or technical processes but across time.

*Many of us have this hang-up about needing to be perfect.*

In this process of depending on and gaining energy from the past while moving in the present heading toward a future that is uncertain and indeterminate, the possibility of mistakes is compounded. Many of us have this hang-up about needing to be perfect, yet when all is perfect the result can seem sterile and disturbing. The philosophy of imperfection requires a different mindset. We find here the imperfection/perfection paradox. Errors become welcome oddities that are then incorporated as normal. Instead of seeing errors as threats, we perceive them as opportunities. Instead of indicating failure, errors can lead us to deeper engagement and success.

❖

## *. . . the presence of failure indicates a willingness to risk.*

❖

In today's business world one of the counter-intuitive methods of seeking a high-quality employee is to discover whether the person has made a significant error or has had defeats. Some companies, in fact, are wary of those who appear not to have failed in some way, for the presence of failure indicates a willingness to risk. Authors Farson and Keyes, in their provocatively-titled book *Whoever Makes the Most Mistakes Wins— The Paradox of Innovation*, state clearly, "To the true innovator, there's no such thing as a mistake." E. (Jay) Phelan, Jr., expands this concept by suggesting that in the context of community, imperfection, not perfection, displays the value of relationship.

We know that the childlike state allows the combination of both perfection and imperfection. It is much less judgmental and more filled with grace than the "adult" disposition of correctness and singularity. Howard Gardner, who has worked much on the concept of multiple intelligences, says that "the challenge to the educator is to keep alive the mind and the sensibility of the young child. Artists and scientists have always known this: Pablo Picasso famously declared, 'I used to draw like Raphael; it has taken me my whole life to learn to draw like a child.'" Samuel Taylor Coleridge talks about "that willing suspension of disbelief for the moment, which constitutes poetic faith." This childlike disposition allows for the momentary suspension of the assumption that opposites cannot coexist, cannot be reconciled by paradox and mystery.

A few years ago I was given a book that I will always cherish, *Harold and the Purple Crayon* by Crockett Johnson. This little book tells the story of Harold, a child with a "magical" purple crayon, a tool that really is the objectification of his imagination. The story begins simply: "One evening, after thinking it over for some time, Harold decided to go for a walk in the moonlight. There wasn't any moon, and Harold needed a moon for a walk in the moonlight. And he needed something to walk on. He made a long straight path so he wouldn't get lost. And he set off on his walk, taking his big purple crayon with him." Harold's imagination creates the needed moon and path. As he goes about on his journey, Harold uses his crayon to construct the world he needs. Johnson wistfully recreates the world of the childlike state that most adults remember. It is one of simplicity, freedom, imagination, and joy. Harold puts the reader into that context which allows for the reconciliation of opposites through the freedom involved in improvisation.

Life is less about control and certainty and more like art, for in reality, life is risky, complicated, and spontaneous, freeing us to embrace mistakes and surprises along the way. Most of the time we are certain that a broken, failed, discarded item is worthless, but being open to possibilities frees us to be creative, a point made concrete through two anecdotes told by Stephen Nachmanovitch. Who would have imagined that old, discarded oars could become something entirely different, even beautiful? An open and creative outlook allowed Antonio Stradivari to make "some of his most beautiful violins from a pile of broken, waterlogged oars he found on the docks in Venice one day." Similarly, what appears to be a failure can become a discovery of great value when imagination is applied. 3M was experimenting with compounds in an effort to produce a strong bonding adhesive, but the bond proved to be weak. At that point someone realized that there might be a virtue to this ineffective adhesive, thereby creating Post-It Notes, one of the company's greatest successes. This serendipitous result came because someone was free to think "outside the box," to violate the rules and to improvise.

Eric Alexander, an amazingly proficient jazz saxophone player, persists in growing as a musician. A self-declared perfectionist, he seeks to play every note perfectly in tune, even though he admits the instrument itself is imperfect. While he has learned how to deal with this "imperfection within perfectionism," he still works for the perfect, knowing all along he will never reach it: "But I've come to realize that the saxophone is such an imperfect instrument that these little impurities actually are interesting, and I welcome them and like them. It's not a synthesizer, so there's no reason to try to make it sound like one. If certain notes are out of tune or more fragile than others, all the better. That's what gives it the human quality. I don't have time to worry about stupid little things, like 'Why did I screw up G-minor on that session?' Once, that would mess me up for a week. Now I don't even care. I've got to go home and change the diapers. Can I just please get three hours of sleep?" There's so much in this admission. There's the acceptance of reality and our humanity. Without losing his desire to play as well as possible, keeping the highest standard, he simultaneously recognizes the limitations of time and energy, the reality of the paradox of perfect and imperfect.

Alexander wasn't wrong, however, in his search for excellence; improvisation can be a way to develop something far more significant. Many believe composed music or composed anything precludes improvisation. Eric Barnhill reminds us that master composers, who today are known only as composers, were additionally involved improvisationally:

> J.S. Bach, while he was alive, was little known as a composer, and his works were criticized for being dense and old-fashioned—but he was renowned as the greatest improviser on the organ in Europe. A famous French organist once came to town to compete against him, and, hearing him improvise while warming up, promptly left town. Bach put improvisation skills at the center of his teaching. Most of his instructional manuals are how-to books in improvisation. He often wrote out several different versions of his most popular pieces, such as the inventions, to show how a student might

improvise on the structure. Handel wrote one treatise on performance—and half of it was devoted to improvising dances and fugues. Mozart was most famous in his day, according to scholars, 'first as an improviser, then as a composer, then as a pianist.' In a famous piano competition in front of the Pope, Mozart and Clementi not only had to improvise in the final round, they had to improvise pieces together. Beethoven became famous in Vienna not as a composer but as an 'astounding' improviser. It was a full ten years that he was famous as an improviser in Vienna before he started to become well-known for his compositions, and he improvised publicly until the end of his life.

Not in any sense exclusive to classical or jazz music, improvisation is a life process, available to all in almost any realm.

Effective improvisation does not come from nowhere, like Athena fully armed from the forehead of Zeus. It entails preparation, which forms the foundation for creative activity. I have a friend who is a trauma expert. Unlike some who become overwhelmed and incapacitated in a crisis, John comes alive and is primed for action. He told me that when he gets a call and has a half hour of driving to the site, he relaxes by playing music and does not think one iota about how to prepare for the impending ordeal. His high level of preparation and training over the years have given him the confidence he needs to approach the situation in a relaxed and open manner. He trusts himself to execute judgment with common sense and to improvise in the moment to provide as much help as possible. When I heard him describe this scenario I was initially shocked, for it sounded counter-intuitive to meet a traumatic event in such a laid-back manner. The more I have thought about it, however, the more sense it makes. He trusts his training. Before arriving at the scene, he goes to a calm place within himself. He is depending on the structure of his background to free him to take charge, instructing, listening, and caring for those hurting. The balance of structure and freedom, of preparation and execution, seems a healthy model that can be applied to organizations, artistic expressions, and relational matters in life.

Being open to innovation and improvisation is a key to success. Often this openness comes as a result of a history of improvisation. Lou Antolihao reports that "Filipinos have developed the 'culture of improvisation,' a way of life that is characterized by adaptation, creativity, and innovation." Peter J. Paris notes a similar situation in Africa: "Westerners visiting anywhere in Africa can be constantly surprised in observing the improvisational work of African auto mechanics repairing engine difficulties with limited tools and few if any spare parts. Such improvisational skills are truly inventive. Since poverty constitutes a basic condition for many improvisational practices, African peoples bestow much praise on the authors of invention because, more often than not, their product represents the creation of something new out of virtually nothing."

When NASA's Apollo 13 systems failed, the ground crew and flight personnel alike were fully open to creativity—improvisation. Normally NASA's structure is based on control, but when they were faced with an extraordinary situation in which they were essentially without the control they normally had, they were fully motivated to improvise. They had to be creative within the available resources. They had unity of purpose. They fortunately knew each element available. Their challenge was somehow to cleverly utilize the available resources and figure out a way to guide the spaceship to earth safely. Fortunately they were successful.

In all the above examples we find people improvising well because they are grounded in knowledge and culture while being open to experimentation and novelty. Nachmanovitch emphasizes this idea of balance between the foundational and the open: "With too little judgment, we get trash. With too much judgment, we get blockage. In order to play freely, we must disappear. In order to play freely, we must have a command of technique. Back and forth flows the dialogue of imagination and discipline, passion and precision. We harmonize groundedness in daily practice with spiritedness in daily stepping out into the unknown."

This is good advice for companies and organizations who want to be distinctive and progressive. While organizations typically value order and control, they also need creativity, which seems to defy control. As Sawyer suggests, "The key to improvised innovation is managing a paradox: establishing a goal that provides a focus for the team—just enough of one so that team members can tell when they move closer to a solution—but one that's open-ended enough for problem-finding creativity to emerge."

This notion of freedom within structure can be seen in this account by Mary Catherine Bateson from *Composing A Life*: "Even in a crazy quilt, the various pieces, wherever they come from, have to be trimmed and shaped and arranged so they fit together, then firmly sewn to last through time and keep out the cold. Most quilts are more ambitious: they involve the imposition of a new pattern. But even crazy quilts are sewn against a backing; the basic sense of continuity allows improvisation."

*While forming the music, I'm simultaneously being formed by the music I'm forming.*

When I improvise musically I also experience the fascinating dialectic of structure and freedom. My creation comes about by exploring freely and knowing it is based on previous experiences. As I explore, I find new sounds, propelled by all I have heard in the past. While forming the music, I'm simultaneously being formed by the music I'm forming. The entire experience of exploring and "fiddling around" entails a response, both to sounds and to the social environment, the audience. If I share my newly-found sounds with someone and it falls flat (a delightfully acceptable and appropriate pun), then I explore differently than if it's a raging success. I am affected/effected by others. As I improvise toward what I think I want to hear, my own background of accumulated sound experiences and the audience interaction become that to which I respond.

Byron Kirk Jones, a preacher and lover of jazz, speaks of veteran saxophonist Sonny Rollin's insights into the improvisational process as a kind of "letting go" where he seems to get outside himself: "Whenever I try to create solos when I'm playing, what I am basically trying to do is blot out my mind as much as possible. Of course, I have already learned the material. After learning the material I try to blot out my mind and let it flow by itself. So I try not to really think too much about what I am playing when I am playing. I sort of have the structure already and then I try to create and let it come by itself." Interviewed by Ben Ratliff, Joshua Redman, a younger sax player who listens extensively to Sonny Rollins, says, "But what Sonny showed me was that you could be completely spontaneous and at the same time have this unerring sense of logic and structure." Fred Frith put the same idea another way: "Logic is for when I'm considering what I might do. Love is for when I'm doing it."

Another confluence in the relational element of improvisation is the issue of autonomy versus interdependence. Several years ago I participated in a demanding hike of Mt. Defiance on the Oregon side of the Columbia River Gorge. It was a one-hundred-degree day and one person brought only about a cup of water even though he knew we would be ascending a 5,000-foot elevation gain. All of us experienced dread, anxiety, and virtually no fun the entire day as we coped with our dehydrated companion. The three of us had never hiked together before. I had expected that each person would bring his own food and beverage. Actually the one who came with almost no water was the person who had hiked this mountain before, several times at that. One hour into the hike and thereafter it became increasingly apparent that the person without ample water was not himself, and as he became progressively more dehydrated the danger of his collapsing was imminent. In contrast, the freedom all three of us would have experienced all day with playfulness and joy was replaced with constant concern and worry. All three of us did make it to the top and back safely, but this took several sacrificial compensatory actions. Structure crumbled as one person's autonomy trumped an otherwise potential of elated interdependence.

Some people view improvising as the opposite of planning, but it is more complicated than that. Improvisation takes place within a social context, each performer being an active participant in the process. It is a complex interplay that is dependent on the nature, expertise, preparation, and history of all involved. Cornel West articulates this complexity in his inimitable way, noting the creative tensions that come into play:

> I use the term 'jazz' here not so much as a term for a musical art form, as for a mode of being in the world, an improvisational mode of protean, fluid, and flexible dispositions toward reality suspicious of 'either/or' viewpoints, dogmatic pronouncements, or supremacist ideologies. To be a jazz freedom fighter is to attempt to galvanize and energize world-weary people into forms of organization with accountable leadership that promote critical exchange and broad reflection. The interplay of individuality and unity is not one of uniformity and unanimity imposed from above but rather of conflict among diverse groupings that reach a dynamic consensus subject to questions and criticism. As with a soloist in a jazz quartet, quintet or band, individuality is promoted in order to sustain and increase the *creative* tension with the group—a tension that yields higher levels of performance to achieve the aim of the collective project."

That same dynamic can be seen in one of the most famous recording sessions ever. In 1959, according to Frank Barrett, Miles Davis handed the musicians "sketches of songs that were written in unconventional modal forms using scales that were very foreign to western jazz musicians at that time. One song, [sic] contained 10 bars instead of the more familiar 8 or 12 bar forms that characterize most standards. Never having seen this music before and largely unfamiliar with the forms, there was no rehearsal. The very first time they performed this music, the tape recorder was running. The result was the album *Kind of Blue*, widely regarded as a landmark jazz recording. When we listen to this album, we are witnessing the musicians approaching these pieces for the first time, themselves discovering new music at the same time that they were inventing it." Miles Davis was very careful in his choice of musicians, a wise aspect of the "structural" element. He hired the most advanced players, those he could trust to handle an innovative protocol. These "cats" knew the jazz canon. They were well-equipped to deal with normal structures, so that when thrown a curve they could move within it. This became clear, as this recording became an instant classic and is still heard around the world today. It exudes freedom and beauty, a natural flow that seems to belie the fact that it had its origins in a huge risk. But that is what improvisation is about—freedom based on preparation and experience.

To decide to live with risk sets up the possibility of tension and vexation. Our desire for control and our unfounded illusion that we can control can lead us away from freedom. Jazz trumpeter Art Farmer believes that *not* needing to control is a way of experiencing freedom. In an interview regarding learning and improvisation he talks about control and freedom:

> Q: Are there times when it comes together and you get a feeling you can realize almost any idea you think of, getting a certain flow going?
>
> AF: Yeah, it usually happens when you're not trying. You know, that's the main thing because the ultimate objective would be to do it when you want to. That's the thing that I'm working on. I'd like to be in command, in control—not just to play something nice at some time that's not when I want to play it.
>
> Q: Are there ways a player can work towards that kind of control, ways of practicing to move along the path toward that ideal?

AF: Well, I think the more you know about harmony, about dealing with harmony and dealing away from harmony, the better off you are—the more things that you have that you can use. But the main problem is to free your mind and I don't know anything you can practice to do that. Because I find with my own playing that whenever I feel any kind of tension, that's when I play the most fundamental things. When I feel ill at ease, my mind just doesn't go out. You know, if I think about what I play under those conditions, they're the most inside things.

## *Improvisation requires control and simultaneously requires release of control.*

Improvisation requires control and simultaneously requires release of control. That paradox is always present in improvisation. For example, in jazz, knowing the harmony means knowing the structure, and that produces control, in the best sense of the term. Owning the structure allows me freedom to express improvisationally within and through it. The more I know, the more I can control. Yet here is the irony: the more I can control, the more I need wisdom in knowing when to give up control. That is the challenge in jazz. Wisdom is knowing when to let go and when to accept an unknown outcome, relinquishing control and trusting mutual influence. As Dorothy Leeds notes, "The issue of control is a complicated topic that includes many gray areas. We want to be in control, but we do not want to be controlling. We want to be independent and spontaneous, but we do not want to be reckless. We want to take control during difficult situations, but relinquish it when necessary. As with other things in life, the goal is balance—to keep a level of control that is not destructive to ourselves or to others, but that we can depend on for strength and support."

As already noted, improvisation always implies a process, a being "in the moment" while moving into an unknown future. That is how the concept of control is related to the matter of adapting to the present circumstances. As that progress occurs, the improviser must always adjust to that change. Adaptation is necessary. Actors learn to portray their characters appropriately by having their characters vary their presentation. As Stanislavski put it, "Each change of circumstance, setting, place of action, time—brings a corresponding adjustment. You adjust yourself differently in the dead of night, alone, from the way you do in daylight and in public. When you arrive in a foreign country you find ways of adapting yourself in a way suitable to the surrounding circumstances."

Paul F. Berliner expands the idea of adaptation to other arts. He notes again that the artist of any kind is working in a changing context, and that the expression necessarily follows the change:

> Artists in many fields experience a creative tension when they explore new lines of thought and interact in unpredictable ways with materials and ideas. A sculptor chipping at a marble block mediates between the initial vision for the sculpture and its evolving shape. Each chisel stroke potentially alters its form in unintended ways or reveals new features in the grain's internal flow that suggests modification of the artwork's design. Similarly, for novelists, writing is not simply an exercise in recording formerly held thoughts, but one for pursuing their unexplored implications. No sooner do authors create characters than they struggle to control them in the face of ever-expanding possibilities for their development and interaction. In the heat of writing, novelists are at times spellbound by their own characters, who, much like the melodies of improvisers, appear to assume lives and voices of their own, revealing

new insights that can shift a work's emphasis in unanticipated ways.

The interplay of adaptation and interpretation applies to not only improvisation but to what transpires when interpreting conventional notated music. Carol Goul and Kenneth Keaton present an argument for this concept: "But is it not the case that a classical performer interpreting a work produces a unique sound event and does so with an element of spontaneity? For instance, two different interpretations of, say, a Bach cello suite will elicit different tempi, bowing, execution of chords, ornamentation . . . .. Moreover, each time one plays a piece or even a phrase, the different nuances can create aesthetically different effects."

Improvisation—in jazz, in art, in life—has much to do, then, with how we deal with the changes in our worlds. While we long for stability and permanence, we recognize that mutability is the order of the day, and so we improvise, we learn how to make music without the score, to pray without the written prayer, to teach a class without notes, to cook without a recipe. We take the risk of letting our right hemispheres develop and join with the left. The joining might be messy at first, but in the end the whole is indeed greater in meaning and expressive communication.

*Part Three*
# Improvisation and
# Dialogue

# CHAPTER SEVEN

# *My Relational Dialogue Journey*

When I was about twelve, my parents had friends over for dinner. This couple seemed rather serious-minded and formal. As was typical, I "took in" the conversation as if a spectator. From my accumulated years of experience in my family, I figured that I was to be seen and not necessarily heard. I sensed that because of my youth I did not have an equal voice in the family or in social situations. Whether true or not, I felt that way; I played it safe and kept myself outside the conversation. That was the reigning belief in childrearing at that time and that is what I learned: children were to pay their dues, prove their worth by becoming adults, and finally earn the right to speak with other grownups.

The dinner was just another time for me to learn my place in society. As an obedient, well-trained child, I remained silent, absorbing the four adults' conversation and behaving respectfully. At one point the guest gentleman looked at me and said, "Still waters run deep." I wasn't sure what he meant—he may have been uncomfortable with my silence, or perhaps he respected me and wanted to hear my thoughts. That I will never know. Because I sensed I didn't quite measure up, I kept quiet. Looking back I see the roots of my perception that I did not have a "voice," that I wasn't worthy to express my thoughts and feelings. I was like Ellison's Invisible Man.

So when might someone find the right moment to go public with his or her thoughts? I don't believe it happens until that person feels safe. There are three options if you don't feel safe: risk, indifference, or silence. You can go out on a limb and speak, hoping to be heard and accepted. You can speak out, not caring what others think or how they react. Or you can remain silent, stifling your voice yet again. In my case, at least, I needed safety. I rarely experienced it growing up. If it was there, I missed it. Honestly, I don't think it was there.

When someone uses something I say to my detriment and demeans me more than once, I am likely to hide or in some way go into protective mode. Because I felt inferior as a human, I became cautious and sheepish, curbing words and thoughts that could have been expressed. I chose for my companions those I felt safe with or who had such strong verbal skills that I could rely on their natural ability to do all the talking.

I don't think I am alone in all these feelings, however. By showing in my own experience how interlinked "safety" and "voice" are, I am hoping that you can explore and understand your own journey to develop a voice. Wounding words and oppressive behaviors or teachings not only hinder the development of a voice but also can be psychologically destructive. Intentional or not, these demeaning actions or words can do much to cause personal hurt and to quench self-expression.

How many of us don't sing, dance, do art, or make a comment about something because we received disparaging remarks at some point? My wife produces amazing flower arrangements, hundreds of them a year. Some of them are requested for a special purpose, but many of them come from deep within herself, they are simply self-expressions that give her joy. It's a passion. She is not an official flower arranger. She has not gone through formal routes to acquire this skill, but she makes absolutely captivating displays that everybody appreciates. What if someone in her past had made a disdainful comment regarding her flower arranging? What if in her childhood some insensitive person had made a callous remark that thwarted her self-concept regarding flowers? Today she might not share her love of flowers and the many arrangements she makes for others.

When we talk about what people say and do, we come to the crux of human relationships, of interpersonal communication. The choices we make have significant and long-lasting consequences. I find this to be particularly true in the teacher-student relationship, for the words and spirit of the teacher have much to do with my learning and with my personal development. I am keenly aware of this dialogic experience, for I am both a student and a teacher. As a private music student myself, having taken lessons from several teachers, I realize that *how* the teacher relates with me can help make me either more fearful or more inspired. In the opposite role, in being a private music teacher, I have learned a great deal that contributes toward healthy dialogue.

While in college I taught reading and playing skills to about twenty-five private piano students. As I developed as a teacher, I discovered that teaching has many similarities with parenting. I believe there are two major facets for both. One is content. You must have something of substance to share. Second is rapport. Most people don't respond well to being commanded; rather, they value the togetherness that a dialogic approach produces. The relationship I developed with students and parents depended on dialogue. My communication skills were in force. I listened to the persons I taught as well as to their parents. These early teaching experiences were ultimately defining my fascination with the process of dialogue.

My private piano teaching stopped when Barb and I went to live on Okinawa. While there I was not involved in teaching; instead, I worked in radio programming as a scriptwriter, newscaster, and announcer. I also traveled to perform on the marimba, did some recording work, and studied mass media. As I mentioned earlier, I met Don Alexander at that time. He and I became great friends, studying the Bible together, talking at length about theology, and considering some of the larger issues of life. Don was extremely loving and perceptive. He had a gift of reconciliation. When he would encounter persons bickering, it wasn't long before the same people were conversing lovingly. Don's love was unconditional; he truly cared for persons.

One day he cared for me in the most spiritual and radical way. He surprised me by coming to the radio station where I worked, a place he had never visited before. Apparently on a mission, Don entered my office and spoke as a prophet to me. He addressed a subject we had discussed before, but I had not yet understood its consequences—about who I was and what that meant. He had many times before asked me, "What do *you* want to do?" I had never really answered that. This was now a turning point for me. Until that time, I had dealt mainly with rules and their implicit or explicit limitations. Now Don came asking me to think and to be real. He was giving me a voice. His love was providing me the safety I had not experienced earlier in my life. Because the time was short and the matter was so important, he came right to the point. Looking me squarely in the eye, he said, "You want it in black and white?" to which I said, "What are you talking about?" I was ready for whatever he was about to say, for I had high respect for him and I trusted him completely. He then stated four unforgettable words: "You are a teacher." He then left.

What was I to do now? I completed my shift on the radio and headed home, thinking seriously about the ramifications of what I had heard. So, I am a teacher. Yes, I *am* a teacher. I agreed, at least conceptually. It was as if it had been sitting at the end of my nose my whole life and I had not seen it. Yet that was all theoretical. Equally powerful were accompanying thoughts and emotions: I am not qualified; I am not worthy to teach (perfectionism rearing itself again). The negative self-talk was strong, but the positive shone more powerfully. Consequently I pursued the goal of being a teacher.

Right away I knew that I wanted to teach college students. My next logical thought was that I had a lot to offer in the field of music. I set my sights on obtaining a graduate degree that would enable me to teach. Within a year Barb and I left Okinawa and moved to Lawrence, Kansas. Headed toward a doctorate in musicology at the University of Kansas, thinking this was an appropriate program for me, I studied pipe organ as my primary instrument and took a full load winter semester, 1970. Whoa! Within the first week of classes I realized this was not the right course of action. I was very impressed by the professors and the rigorous academic expectations. At the same time I deciphered how they applied their passion of music by studying *about* music and I applied my passion by *performing* music. I was in the wrong type of degree program for who I was and what I wanted to become. Depression ensued. Not knowing what in the world to do, having romanticized the return to formal learning, I couldn't have been more discouraged in the educational quest.

I called my friends and asked for advice. That was an amazing set of conversations. In such dire circumstances and feeling stranded in the middle of the country, I called one friend in Chicago with what must have seemed to him an SOS. Howie and his wife, Vivian, drove down. He and I talked about my dilemma for about thirty-six hours nonstop one weekend. I'm quite certain that I did ninety percent of the talking with Howie's empathetic ear receiving my pain and extensive explanations. Hearing myself think aloud about my predicament with a respected human being listening carefully and lovingly, I came to grips with what I needed to do. Interestingly, Howie never suggested anything. Instead, as he listened to me so carefully, I was able to sort through my tendency to choose the least joyous route in life, thinking that I would gain merit through such suffering. At last, I awakened to another script, that of pursuing life within my strengths.

The next two wonderful years I was a student in Chicago concentrating on percussion. One of those years I taught percussion one long day a week at Harper College. From this experience I realized that students very much appreciated my giving them voice through safety and my recognizing their importance as human beings. Put another way, they realized that they were not simply percussion students but they were persons who were interested in playing music through percussive means; they were first and foremost human beings. This fortified my disposition toward dialogical teaching: a two-way approach with me serving as a facilitator for the sake of student learning.

The next stage of teaching opportunities took place in Portland, Oregon. For several years I practiced my dialogical teaching mostly by giving private music lessons. Occasionally I had the opportunity to teach college as an adjunct, allowing me to apply my teaching style to groups of students. To develop my teaching prowess I regularly attended pedagogical sessions, conferences, and workshops. Most of these offered progressive, rather than traditional, teaching concepts and tips. This is what I was seeking, for as a kid I had left too many music lessons crying, not at all what I wanted to be causing in my students.

Since my upbringing was loaded with the modeling of iron-fisted teaching (traditional), I needed additional reminders of how to teach with a high respect for the student in a trusting, healthy process (progressive). Workshops I attended pointed to the importance of *how* we teach while not at all losing sight of *what* we are teaching. In no way less rigorous, this treatment of students was coinciding with my increased understanding of emotion. The growing research in social psychology that was making in-roads into communication was beginning to influence my teaching. I was learning how to make "I" statements instead of "you" statements, thereby avoiding the confrontational and accusatory attitude implied by that rhetoric. All of us deal with the same issues of discipline, self-control, play, making decisions, and so on. Teachers are not exempt, yet the way some teachers (and parents) speak to others can be easily taken as belittling. I wanted to avoid such behaviors. Another way I was learning to relate with students was to cut any blaming tactics and instead simply assert something as positively as possible. Rather than point out what was wrong, especially in a harsh, demeaning manner as if the person should know better, I would say, "Next time, I expect such and such."

I also learned about assertive leadership and how it provides better security, whether addressing one person or many. Instead of attempting to please everyone by intentionally being vague with my expectations and instructions, I learned to be forthright. I would state clearly and confidently what was going to happen and how it would happen. I found that people ultimately appreciate this straightforward approach more than one that is vague and general. I began to realize that in being ambiguous and casual I was trying to be everyone's friend; the result, however, was confusing and ineffective. My change in style started to have real effects on my students.

As I reflected on my teaching, I began to see that a central component in its success was my emphasis on dialogue. Because I had seen the importance of safety and voice in my experience, I began to emphasize dialogue in my own life. I found myself organizing small groups with the intention of bringing people together for meaningful conversation. Ever since age twenty-five I had found myself in one or two small groups regularly. These meetings enabled the participants to share their feelings and thoughts safely and help them develop their voice in the presence of friends. I realized that I had to continue that sort of activity, both personally and pedagogically.

*Meaningful social interaction and mutual support are essential for both improvisation and dialogue.*

Relational and purposeful dialogue can be viewed as a connection of souls. This creates an environment where all participants have equal voices. Everyone listens. The goal for such conversations is to produce collaboration that is interactive and spontaneous, dialogue that inspires creative thinking. All are considered co-learners. This attitude stimulates a good spirit among all participants. When people are relaxed, they are more apt to be themselves, to be authentic. These characteristics parallel what's involved in improvisation. Meaningful social interaction and mutual support are essential for both improvisation and dialogue.

Collective improvisation has a dual dynamic, it both involves and affects each person in some manner all the time. Understanding this duality, jazz musician Wynton Marsalis reflects on the power of dialogue he experienced as a developing young man:

> Back then, these two revelations—*the importance of expressing the core of your unique feelings* and *the willingness to work things out with others*—gave me more than I needed to address the increasingly complex personal relationships that can be unbearable for a teenager. On a

basic level, this music led me to a deeper respect for myself. In order to improvise something meaningful, I had
to find and express whatever I had inside of me worth
sharing with other people. But at the same time it led
me to a new awareness of others, because my freedom
of expression was directly linked to the freedom of others on the bandstand. I had something to say, and so did
they. *The freer they were, the freer I could be, and vice
versa.* To be heard demanded that we also listened to
one another. Closely. And to sound good we had to trust
one another.

True dialogue must exhibit trust, which then develops trust, a trust that
is essential to both the individual and the group.

In 1990, I enrolled in a workshop titled "Writing to Teach Critical
Inquiry." Even though I didn't realize it at first, this experience was to
change my professional and personal life radically. For one week, eight
hours a day, in a learning community of fourteen under the tutelage of an
English professor, I was stimulated by the expectation of transparency.
Even though I generally love such openness and interacting directly, this
process required that we read to others what we wrote right then—no
fixing or dressing up. As this level of sharing took place I experienced a
vibrant, joyful state. I found deep satisfaction and contentment in being
known by otherwise complete strangers and in getting to know them.
Because I was thrown into freewriting (continuous writing without regard to spelling, grammar, and word choice), what did get on the paper
was my heart. In freewriting any form of correcting, editing and cen-
suring is disallowed. Instead, realizing I could always later make those
changes for a better presentation, I could relax. As we went around the
circle several times daily, always reading our spontaneously-written as-
signments, I noticed how acceptance was essential. No one said "good"
or "bad." In fact, the writings were simply received without feedback,
in whatever form they existed. I found this freeing. From the point of

acceptance would eventually come ideas for expansion or deletion and directions to consider moving the writing onward, but this always began from a point of "as is" first.

Frankly, I'm not sure I had ever before experienced this accepting response to any type of performance in life. It permitted an unbelievable safety for conversation about what we had just written. Rather than immediately getting into how each piece was written, we were free to discuss the content. From this I learned how important and powerful safety was for dialogue. Additionally, I had rarely experienced such camaraderie with others, even though they were quite unlike myself in background and beliefs. The differences did not matter. We were free to be authentic and we were completely accepted without criticism. What a model for life! I found it to be extremely gratifying. This weeklong experience fortified and expanded my appreciation for dialogue.

Another defining time in my dialogical development occurred in 1999. While on sabbatical I observed classes from around thirty colleges and met with the respective professors to discuss teaching ideas. I had selected these professors because their students had rated them highly. These were stellar experiences for me. When I was in the classroom my goal was to observe the professor's leadership style, the actions of the students and the professor, and the interaction of students and the professor. My later reflections helped me see more clearly how the professor influenced the class. Three factors were always present within the sixty-six classes I visited: The professor was overflowing with passion for the subject; the professor cared about the students and their learning; the class was interactive.

Approaching this sabbatical quest with an open mind, simply wanting to see many educational processes, I was intrigued when my hunches about effective teaching and learning were confirmed. I noted that in these stimulating classroom experiences the professor was a dynamic facilitator of learning who formed a learning community. In essence I witnessed "dialogue education" where the unique perspective of each learner was recognized and valued. In contrast to "domination education" where each class member is expected to conform to the professor's ideas, dialogic teaching allows all voices to be heard. Even when student ideas may seem far-fetched, a learning community within the professor's careful and sensible guidance works together to determine which ideas can actually be supported. This style re-creates the old idea of the university—a community of learners humbly seeking knowledge and working together to achieve as a group what no one person could ever achieve alone. Within this framework students do not compete against one another; rather, success is acknowledged as everyone achieves his or her own potential. Within this perspective, students are free to work toward their peers' success as well as their own. Describing this kind of attitude Martha Nussbaum notes the imaginative process needed here, "the ability to think what it might be like to be in the shoes of a person different from oneself, to be an intelligent reader of that person's story, and to understand the emotions and wishes and desires that someone so placed might have. The narrative imagination is not uncritical, for we always bring ourselves and our own judgments to the encounter with another . . . understanding we will also judge that story in the light of our own goals and aspirations."

Valuing the co-learner is paramount in all of life, not just in small groups or education. Jesus seems to suggest such a point when he implies that all of us are fellow learners under the tutelage of God: "But you are not to be called 'Rabbi,' for you have one Teacher, and you are all brothers. And do not call anyone on earth 'father,' for you have one Father, and he is in heaven. Nor are you to be called instructors, for you have one Instructor, the Messiah." (Matthew 23:8-10) To see each other as learners does more than instill value in the individual by uniting and equalizing all in the endeavor. It establishes relationship among the learners and between learners and the teacher. Moreover, it emphasizes the process of education involved in our life together.

All relationships can move toward participatory engagement within an environment of co-learning. When I see myself as a creature, the result of a Creator, I adopt an attitude of humility, not hubris, and acknowledge that communally we are sojourners. Instead of engaging in a consumer mentality and passive reception, co-learning is both dynamic and participatory for all. Such mutuality allows for sharing who we are and what is occurring with and within us, all the while respecting the differences between us. Everyone is encouraged to give context to what they are saying by telling their stories, and then listeners can give feedback. Such feedback is intended to provide understanding and mutual support, never control.

A while back I posed the following question to my Faith, Living, and Learning class: "What have you learned through this class, which is about faith, living, and learning?" In response a student wrote:

> Going back over my notes, I find things that I have written that reveal a new level of understanding that I had not before reached. I've learned that each person's experience can help me to make sense of my experience. Listening to the stories that people would tell in class in many ways showed how I'm not the only one who is going through the things that I'm going through. I am also able to expand my ideas based on the ideas of others. Hearing people say things that I would never have thought of on my own gives me a new perspective on things. I also learned that even though I may feel uncomfortable talking about what I think, talking things out in small groups can be helpful in helping me better understand what I think. Verbally articulating my thoughts allows me to see if they make sense.

For me this person "gets it." This student, by being engaged, both learned and reflected on the experience. All of this took place in the context of the community, which can be as small as two persons or as large as hundreds. Transformation can result from the reciprocal efforts and openness.

The potential to experience transformation through dialogue can occur within many situations, whether at the dining table, in a classroom, in a quilting circle, or while hiking. Creating safety to allow voice is key. This experience is based in the root belief that all persons involved are co-learners and that mutual respect is essential and demonstrable. All facets of dialogue apply to the leader as well. By whatever title—coach, teacher, parent, guide, etc.—the person initiating dialogical energy lives by the same guidelines as everyone else. Only with this key equality can the dialogue function productively, resulting in interaction experienced freely and spontaneously.

# CHAPTER EIGHT

## *What Dialogue Is and Is Not*

Let's begin this chapter by imagining a scenario. A friend invites you to go to a jazz club together. You arrive at the club after a long, hard day at work, weary and distracted by all the demands on you and your time. It is 7:00 p.m., an hour before the show is to begin, but enough time to share a meal together. As you enter the room, you notice what you had heard about the place—it is really "cool," with lighting set low, tables placed strategically, walls filled with pictures and other items linked to the jazz players who had been to the club previously. The wait staff is bustling around attentively but without intrusion. You order your meal and wait for the entire experience to begin. By 7:30 you are well into eating and digesting, not only food but the day and elements of your life. Your friend is an attentive, caring listener. Already you are feeling more relaxed about the day's challenges. The musicians begin ambling in, getting out their horns and chatting amongst themselves; you sense the energy in the house. Your mood is shifting toward the mood of the musicians, who you notice are humoring one another with anecdotes and sharing thoughts about their lives since the last gig together. You also notice how each of them deals with warming up his instrument, making adjustments, and in general getting ready. They are revealing anticipation, faith, hope, and love. It is clear to everyone—these musicians deeply desire to make music together.

At 8:00 the music begins, the patrons perk up, and you begin to focus your attention on the musicians and the music they are making. Caught up in the evening, you sit back and go for a ride. You also become aware of another level of experience as you allow yourself to think about what is occurring around and within you. You notice that the feel of the music comes as much from the relationships among members of the group as from the sounds they are making—and maybe they are inextricably linked. The musicians are communicating with each other through eye contact, through gestures, and through very brief comments. The communication contributes to the unity and the spirit of the band itself. Each of the players is an outstanding musician, accomplished on his instrument. Yet here they have begun to mold themselves into a group, a unified and organic whole. Each member surrenders himself to the whole and to the music. One steps up and begins his improvisational solo, responding to what had gone on before and fitting into the musical conversation. He speaks, through his instrument, to the others and to the audience. Then he is done and shortly another leads the conversation. Back and forth they go, relating musically and harmoniously.

The set ends a short hour and a half later, and you have a chance to reflect on what you have experienced. You note that in the improvisational music you had seen individuals relating to each other in joy and purpose. The band members had been exhibiting characteristics endemic to jazz improvisation, dialogue, and healthy living in general: togetherness, common purpose, commitment, risk-taking, mutual respect and support, listening to one another, stepping out with courage, geniality, engagement, playfulness, expectancy, desire, passion, humility, storytelling, and, in short, seeking to create shared meaning. The result was cohesiveness with soul. The music was beyond the sum of the parts. It was mysteriously happening, unfolding so naturally and yet so skillfully. It was meaningful dialogue.

It is fairly common for people—experts as well as common listeners—to talk about jazz in terms of everyday verbal interaction. That isn't unusual, because some of the same relational phenomena are present, whether it is one instrumentalist interacting with another musically or one person interacting with another conversationally. It is all about dialogue, a term that we need to consider a bit more fully as we think about the interrelatedness of faith, improvisation, and dialogue and as we consider the relational aspects of conversation.

Susan Scott's cleverly-titled book, *Fierce Conversations*, includes a "story of the man who visits a Zen master. The man asks, 'what truths can you teach me?' The master replies, 'Do you like tea?' The man nods his head, and the master pours him a cup of tea. The cup fills and the tea spills. Still the master pours. The man, of course, protests, and the master responds, 'Return to me when you are empty.' The lesson here is that we need to empty ourselves of our preconceived beliefs in order to be open to a broader, more complex reality." Conversing is a kind of "emptying" as we interact with another, learning, revising, and opening our thinking to our involvement with others.

Juanita Brown says, "What if humans are in conversation the way fish are in water?" True, conversation is the normal experience of human beings. In everyday life we are frequently involved in conversation with the many others we meet during our day. Using our essential linguistic competence, we engage them to communicate, to please, to request, to move, etc. We use language and play with language in our verbal relating to people. This activity is quite similar to the music improvisation we have considered earlier. If we have basic linguistic competence and some self-awareness, we can create meaningful expressions spontaneously and freely. We can also respond to the conversational interplay of the other. In the process, we deal with the risk and the fear that we might be misunderstood, that we might, as it were, play a wrong note. We also, of course, live in the hope that we find the perfect phrase to communicate our thoughts and feelings. In that emotional and linguistic tension we are dealing with the elements of child-play, creative interaction and not performance of set pieces. Unlike a performance of something already created that needs to be interpreted suitably, improvisation and conversation have in common the "where it goes it goes" trademark.

❖

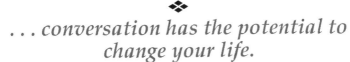

*. . . conversation has the potential to change your life.*

❖

Preben Friis says much the same from the perspective of theater: "I begin to see it as the social interaction emerging between people all the time. Our conversations and bodily communication as gesturing and responding are an ongoing improvisation created moment by moment. When we improvise, we are spontaneously responding to each other's gestures, and thus we do not know the full meaning of what we are doing until we have done it. The meaning emerges through the process of having intentions, acting and getting responses. This is a social process, where we are creating meaning together in what we are doing in the act of doing it." This is why conversation has the potential to change your life. Conversation is more than about relationship; it is relationship.

Sociologist Erving Goffman extends Friis's idea by noting the enormous array of responses available in conversation: "Although any conversational move is appreciably determined by the preceding moves of other participants, and appreciably determines the moves that follow, still much looseness is found; for at each juncture a whole range of actions seems available to the individual, and his particular selection is a matter of free choice." I am always amazed when analyzing a conversation how one person's comment can turn the direction entirely when it could have continued its particular flow for another five minutes. This give and take reminds me of children's play: the game could be going along when suddenly one of the children suggests another activity and, often without hesitation, the others join in. It seems simply to be a matter of an initiator role, just as in conversation. It's loose enough that the respondent readily accepts the change of focus, going with the flow.

Conversation, which literally means "to turn with," implies that the participants keep together with each other, turning together through the linguistic journey. In conversation there is freedom to change course, and there is not necessarily any expectation of closure. Because there is unity of movement there is no one necessarily in charge. The flow of conversation has its own course, with unpredictable rhythms and constant turns. Collaboration is essential to the progress of conversation, for the dynamic interchange always leads onward together.

Conversationalists vary rhythmically. Some speak often and keep the pace of a conversation moving. Others listen deeply and quietly and rarely speak. In a book simply titled *Conversation*, Theodore Zeldin notes, "One of the most memorable conversationalists in history, the French diplomat Talleyrand, who suffered from a lonely upbringing and a physical handicap, would often sit through a party without saying a word, but then suddenly come out with a sentence which people said was the sort they never forget. What matters is whether you are willing to think for yourself, and to say what you think." Whether it's heavy or very light, conversation is significant to being human. There is something beautiful when a neighbor stops by and a conversation ensues, especially when there's no agenda—it's what is termed as "neighborly."

Keith Sawyer links "conversations" and "dialogues" in remarking on the creative energy and unexpected outcomes from these activities: "The most creative conversations are like improvisational theater dialogues; each speaker reinterprets what was said before and builds on it in a new direction so that unexpected creativity emerges from the group." In conversation one statement builds on the former, leading to a conclusion none of the participants could have foreseen completely. Sawyer likens this to improvisational theater because of its emphasis on listening to the other person(s) and responding in order to continue the flow. The semantics of these terms—conversation and dialogue—can get blurry. My interest is to explore the similarities and differences between conversation and dialogue. Conversation is more casual and dialogue more intentional and purposeful. The goal is for the relaxed, safe, natural, and casual elements of conversation to remain in a dialogue. The distinctive of dialogue would be that it has a center, but not sides, whereas conversation would not necessarily have a center or sides.

Until the 1980s psychologist Jerome Bruner had thought of learning as essentially an unaccompanied activity. He came "increasingly to recognize that most learning in most settings is a communal activity, a sharing of the culture." In gaining other perspectives we become aware of different possibilities for understanding, thereby helping us think, imagine, and be creative beyond the boundaries shaped by our traditions and our limitations. Humans, it seems, do not change alone, or not as much as occurs through relationship. Peter Senge has written about this: "It is most accurate to think of openness as a characteristic of relationships, not of individuals. At some level, it makes no sense to say, 'I am an open person.' The same person will experience genuine openness with some people and not with others. In this sense, like David Bohm's concept of dialogue, openness emerges when two or more individuals become willing to suspend their certainty in each other's presence. They become willing to share their thinking and susceptible to having their thinking influenced by one another. And, as Bohm points out, in a state of openness, they gain access to depths of understanding not accessible otherwise." The musicians at the jazz club were listening to the full group while participating so they could "say something." Having the whole picture, the context, seems paramount for a successful musical or verbal dialogue, just as being open is essential for responding creatively.

## *Openness is a resolve to listen without censure.*

Openness is a resolve to listen without censure. In much of society, closed, prejudicial thinking is prevalent. For example, I was raised in Southern California. From my upbringing I somehow picked up and believed that I lived in the center of the world, that "our" way was "the" way. I was fifteen when I was in Europe for five weeks, my first time away from my dominant culture. Until getting away to another culture, I had assumed all cultures were or should be like "my" culture. However, I learned from the German family with whom I stayed that my crew cut, then fashionable in the U.S., was associated with being a suspicious, potentially dangerous person in their culture. They assumed I was a threat until they got to know me as a person. They had me categorized as a "bad" person. This was my early exposure to such prejudiced categorical thinking. From this experience I learned that relationships—in this case, relationships with people in a different culture—can do much to free a person from old assumptions and enable the person to develop new ways of seeing and responding. I was getting my first dose of pluralism as a way to view life, whereas previously I had been locked into my view as "the" view. Or, as George Kunz says, "We step out of our own perspective in order to enter the experience of the Other."

By entering the world of the Other, we expand our own world, and paradoxically the world of the Other is also enlarged. It is a process of creating a "common reality," of meaning-making, as George Kunz argues:

> Dialogue involves an exchange of information, ideas, and affect with another for the broader and deeper knowledge of the partners and for the common stock of knowledge. Dialogue is the power of cooperation in the free flow of knowledge, especially for an understanding of the different perspectives of the partners. The word "dialogue" is made up of dia- ("across") + legein ("talk"). Dialogue is the mutual exchange of descriptions of realities to form a common reality. In dialogue, we not only increase each one's information, we also modify the knowledge each originally held. We learn what the other knew, we become more aware of what we each previously knew, and we learn the connections between the two. From the dialogue between cooperative partners, the ego can also reach out to others in dialogue. The network of conversations becomes the arena for the development of society.

*Dialogue and improvisation share the complex component of simultaneity.*

Dialogue and improvisation share the complex component of simultaneity. In both, the roles of listener and speaker, of soloist and band, intermix. In dialogue one person listens and the other speaks, but the listening is not passive. Rather, the listener is engaged in intense active listening so that he can respond intelligently and sensitively to what was said, not with what he had intended to say. Often in pseudo-dialogue, an individual is just waiting to say what he wanted to say before the other person started talking. When an opening occurs, he just jumps in with his original point, regardless of what had been said. That isn't real dialogue; it is neither sensitive nor productive. In a dialogue, one is clearly listening, then composing responses, and communicating in a way that considers the contexts of the listeners.

Applying full attention, whether speaking or listening, implies a caring stance, which is more likely to produce an empathetic response. If so, it's more difficult to berate the other person. Deborah L. Flick says, "Usually as we come to truly understand what is going on from the other person's standpoint, it becomes difficult to maintain a position of criticism and blame. Blame and criticism recede along with anger, giving way to a willingness to collaborate on discovering new possibilities for dealing with the situation." Understanding another person's point of view does not necessarily mean you agree, nor does it infringe on your own beliefs and values. With cognizance of your own boundaries, hearing others allows you to know what they think and how they operate.

Those in the business world find this dialogic model useful because they recognize that the possibility for innovation increases with a relational, improvisational approach; in this paradigm members are better able to absorb each person's ideas and insights. One person's idea can be used by others for dialogical interplay. Keith Sawyer likens creative collaboration to improvisational theater: "No single actor comes up with the big picture, the whole plot. The play emerges bit by bit. Each actor, in each line of dialogue, contributes a small idea. In theater, we can see this process on stage; but with an innovative team, outsiders never see the long chain of small incremental ideas that lead to the final innovation. Without scientific analysis, the collaboration remains invisible. Successful innovations happen when organizations combine just the right ideas in just the right structure."

The value of increasing one's available perspectives, especially in problem-solving contexts, can be seen in this story from Cynthia Barton Rabe:

> A waiter, a fitness instructor, and a lawyer see a woman slip in a puddle of water in a busy restaurant. The woman is unhurt and the restaurant owner assumes he simply needs to be faster to mop up spills on the floor. But when each of the three witnesses is asked what problem the restaurant needs to address, they all give a very different response.
>
> Waiter: The problem is that the restaurant needs to hire more wait-staff so spills resulting from rushed service can be avoided.
>
> Fitness Instructor: The problem is that the restaurant needs to replace its slippery floors that provide more traction.
>
> Lawyer: The problem is that the restaurant needs to limit its liability the next time this happens by posting signs telling patrons to watch their step.
>
> Whether any of these perspectives is better than the owner's is up to him. But without exposure to them, he can't even make the call. Obviously this is an example of the benefit of interacting with people who have different mindsets. But people can train themselves to adopt different mindsets, at least to an extent. In this story, although the owner's first response was to be faster with a mop, it's likely that if he were asked to 'think like a lawyer,' he would have to come up with something similar to what the lawyer in this story suggested.

Encountering diverse ideas and viewpoints can produce fear, a sense of insufficiency, or the anxiety that comes from loss of control. On the other hand, the result could be excitement, a love of pluralism, and the sense of enlargement that comes with seeing potential. The key to experiencing the positive possibilities is an openness to diversity. Once a person encounters a context of trust and safety, he is free to recognize honestly that he needs, and desires, even more perspectives. Analogously, several persons working on a jigsaw puzzle can see the whole picture and each piece from a different perspective; consequently the process of putting the puzzle together becomes much easier. So, too, in problem-solving: if several persons work together in dialogue, the multiple perspectives can produce a more creative solution more quickly. The implication is that other persons' thinking can improve your thinking.

For some, working with others by listening, receiving, and incorporating others' inputs is a natural way of life. For others, that type of openness challenges their ego, causing them to react with skepticism and fear. Moreover, the idea of open-ended conversations can annoy some persons because they feel the process itself is a waste of time—no final "best" outcome is achieved. True dialogue, however, stresses the value of relationship over rational certainty, process over product; it argues for openness as a productive ongoing disposition. If relationships are primary, then when we share openly, the dialogue will go on, each participant being valued. The advantage to this stance is that it allows all involved to use the differences to create something new. Privileging creative tension and ongoing dialogue allows a more complete picture to unfold.

Sharon Daloz Parks speaks of this mode of seeing the world in terms of complex meaning-making, of the ways in which the individual deals with the multiple possibilities of objects:

> The mind does not passively receive the world but rather acts upon every object and every experience to compose it. This composing activity occurs even at the level of basic perception. For example,

when we perceive a tree, we compose it, organizing its various parts into a whole—branches, leaves, trunk, roots, textures, colors, height, breadth, and whatever we may know of the intricate systems by which it is nourished or threatened through the seasons of its existence. Though we may all encounter the same tree, each of us composes a different one. Moreover, in interaction with the tree we compose, we each make different meaning of it. Some of us see the subject of a poem; others see a lucrative number of board feet; and still others see a source of shade, shelter, or a threat in a strong wind.

## *Differences, diversity, and variations are stimulating for some, threatening for others.*

Differences, diversity, and variations are stimulating for some, threatening for others. Some find a stimulus attractive while others find that same stimulus ludicrous. Improvisation and dialogue expect multiplicity of outcomes. In improvisation and dialogue the guiding term is "unforeseen." Much of life incorporates what improvisation and dialogue represent—freedom and unknown outcomes. Control and certainty become the antithetical forces. From the world of psychotherapy, David Ricco says, "Control happens when we force our own view or plan on someone else: 'I am attached to a particular outcome and am caught in the need to fix, persuade, advise, or change you.'" Control is in opposition to the freedom, expectancy, and unpredictability of dialogue. Instead of viewing life issues as propositional, this more open approach looks at them through a relational lens. With dialogue it's about questions, and questions imply an attitude of humility.

The relationship inherent in dialogue does not determine a set number of participants. There must be at least two, and the maximum is limited only by the number that can be involved in conversation. What is important, however, is that in talking about dialogue we are talking about group behavior. David Bohm posits three assertions critical to dialogue:

1. Hold assumptions without judgment. Suspend judgment in order to get the fullest context, in order to understand. Do not cut off anything.

2. Hold high regard for others.

3. A facilitator is needed for a group to hold the context, getting all persons involved and owning the process and outcomes. The facilitator understands the ramifications of the ego process, therefore keeps the group away from such potential fragmentation.

Arnold Mindell reminds us why it is significant that dialogue is involved with group behavior when he discusses the dynamics of the group: ". . . the majority of people deal with tensions in a group by one of three means: repressing the tensions and trying to be nice to one another; analyzing the tensions and trying to change ourselves or others; getting into the tensions and hurting one another." Dialogue becomes a positive way of dealing with those tensions by creating a space of openness where the parties can listen and learn. But in order for dialogue to be productive, those involved must follow processes that are safe and productive. Parker Palmer suggests some rules for group dynamics, rules that correspond to good dialogue: "No fixing, no saving, no advising, no setting each other straight."

When we come together to talk, to be with one another, to have dialogue, process is exceedingly significant. The way in which we treat one another is a central component of the entire interaction. We should respond the way we would want others to respond—honestly. When we are sharing from our heart, we are tenderly vulnerable. When our essence emanates viscerally, without the checks of the rational mind, extra respect is in order, for we are declaring ourselves with little protection, intentionally. An open, trusting spirit conveys a unified attitude, similar to that of a flock of birds exhibiting freedom while maintaining cohesiveness. Bees also have this behavior. David Borgo observes, "Colonies of bees have fascinated observers for millennia with their ability to move around with apparent abandon yet at the same time to display a collective sense of purpose." I am suggesting that we humans emulate the birds and the bees. They are working together as one unit, even though they are separate bees.

We can also define "dialogue" as *improvised human interchange.* Seen from this point of view, dialogue in human communication follows the process of jazz improvisation. When a group member offers a statement or even a feeling, the other group members accept it at face value. Regardless of possibly wanting to push against what is being revealed, group members at this point simply allow the energy to develop from the first person's contribution. Nothing is suggested that would undermine the initial person's premise. This requires a very open listening manner as the group considers multiple perspectives simultaneously in order to obtain the full story. Finally, as each speaker takes a turn at offering a statement with other group members responding with acceptance, the group is able to construct a whole and to learn what the gestalt of the group truly is. Gerzon suggests that this process is "an inquiry-based, trust-building way of communicating that maximizes the human capacity to bridge and to innovate."

The dialogic process of meaning-making demands engagement from all involved, as Daniel Yankelovich observes: "Dialogue turns out to be a highly specialized form of discussion that imposes a rigorous discipline on the participants." For example, if in a dialogue I say, "How are you?" you might give two different responses: "OK" or "I'm feeling great, because I just finished reading the novel I had been enjoying for many weeks." The first stifles dialogue; the second encourages it.

What a difference attitude and involvement make! Instead of working on a retort, a defensive or offensive response, we invest in the other's point of view, the result being new understanding. Yankelovich identifies some of the benefits from this approach: ". . . when dialogue is done skillfully, the results can be extraordinary: long-standing stereotypes dissolved, mistrust overcome, mutual understanding achieved, visions shaped and grounded in shared purpose, people previously at odds with one another aligned on objectives and strategies, new common ground discovered, new perspectives and insights gained, new levels of creativity stimulated, and bonds of community strengthened."

Dialogue strengthens and stimulates community by reinforcing a sense of commonality. As with the flock of birds or swarm of bees, there is shared purpose and understanding. The interaction between humans is more complex, however, for the anxious desire to protect the ego can get in the way of cooperation and union. Dialogue mitigates this resistance, though, by allowing for autonomy even while it is privileging interdependence.

The process of dialogue, then, is an important part of building and strengthening a group, a team. George Kunz develops the significance of the interplay of the individual and the group in this dynamic: "Functioning as an inclusive team requires *interdependent collaboration through communication.* Interdependent collaboration is nourished by mutual trust. It is further supported by membership on the team being a strong enough source of social identity and pride that one is prepared to subordinate one's individual needs to achieving the purpose and goals of the team." The mutuality of real dialogue serves to avoid a rigid adversarial stance. The challenge is to hang onto the beautiful characteristics of the child while maturing into interdependence and responsibility as adults.

On the other hand, debate differs greatly from dialogue. In debate there is no common purpose and no mutuality. There is a clear loser. There is a clear winner. I have a friend with whom I used to play racquetball. When we got to our club and entered the racquetball court, everything changed. I put on my "game face" and prepared for battle. I was not about to let my partner get points because I needed to be nice to him. It was respectful battle that included power, control, endurance and concentration. After we left the court, things were different; they returned to "normal." The game was about competition, and I understood fully that if I would win, my good friend would lose. The game was a debate; our friendship at all other times was a dialogue.

While it is helpful to distinguish between debate and dialogue, it is even more important to find ways of emphasizing dialogue as an attitude, and one that needs to temper everything, even debate. Mark Gerzon offers these helpful distinctions:

❖ In Debate the assumption is that there *is* a right answer and that you have it. In Dialogue the assumption is that many people have pieces of the answer.

❖ In Debate participants try to prove the other side wrong, a combative stance. In Dialogue participants work together toward common understanding, a collaborative stance.

❖ In Debate the listening has its purpose in finding flaws to make counter-arguments. In Dialogue the listening has its purpose in finding meaning with a central purpose to understand.

❖ In Debate the thrust is in defending. In Dialogue the thrust is in revealing.

❖ In Debate the emphasis is in seeing two sides of an issue. In Dialogue the emphasis is in seeing all sides of an issue.

❖ In Debate you are defending your own views against those of others. In Dialogue you are admitting that others' thinking can improve your own.

❖ In Debate you are searching for flaws and weaknesses in others' positions. In Dialogue you are searching for strengths and value in others' position.

❖ In Debate you are seeking a conclusion or vote that ratifies your position. In Dialogue you are discovering new options and not seeking closure.

There may indeed be situations where strong debate is needed, but in general the value of dialogue is paramount, especially insofar as it enhances human relationships.

The unknown, open-ended outcomes at the outset of a dialogue create a strong potential for "flow" and serendipity in the entire process. The relational elements enhance the probability for creativity. When people are relaxed rather than anxious, enjoying each other rather than fearing each other, the potential to work together to accomplish goals is strengthened. That context facilitates dialogue; dialogue fosters collaboration; and collaboration often allows goals to be accomplished that otherwise might not have been met.

The primacy of collaboration flies in the face of our past assumptions and myths. Our culture seems to value the Lone Ranger over the posse approach. Keith Sawyer notes, "We're drawn to the image of the lone genius whose mystical moment of insight changes the world. But the lone genius is a myth; instead, it's group genius that generates breakthrough innovation. When we collaborate, creativity unfolds across people; the sparks fly faster, and the whole is greater than the sum of its parts." Sawyer's message comes from studying two improvising ensembles, jazz and theater, where he witnessed creativity from everyone's active participation. He noted how each person drew energy from the others, thereby creating an energy level significantly higher than the sum of the energies of the individuals. He saw a particular application of this principle in the story of the Wright Brothers, who invented and flew the first powered airplane. "The Wright brothers," he observes, "lived together, ate together, and discussed their project every day. Their collaboration was visible to everyone around them, and it speaks from every page of their journals." What the Wright brothers were able to do was the result of incredible communication through purposeful conversation and dialogue. Because of strong interdependence and mutual respect, these brothers brought about innovation at a high level.

Admittedly this style of living requires trust, both in oneself and in others. Through a relaxed conversational mode and with purposeful and expectant dynamics of dialogue, this outlook allows and encourages feedback from others. Everyone involved can work together to discover creative solutions rather than becoming defensive. Mutual interdependence provides a foundation for productive collaboration that ultimately will bring joy through freedom.

# CHAPTER NINE

# *Dialogue As Confluence*

Ole gets a car phone. He's on his way home on the freeway and calls Lena: "I am calling you from the freeway on my new car phone." Lena answers, "Be careful, Ole, because on the radio they say some nut is driving the wrong way on the freeway." And Ole says, "One nut—heck, there are hundreds of them!"

Communication?! Confluence?! Dialogue?? When we open our mouths and others open their ears, and when all parties are applying their best skills, we still may not fully comprehend what is being communicated. As the prison warden says in *Cool Hand Luke*, "What we have here is a failure to communicate." Communication is always extremely challenging because it is a human activity, and we are all too human. The image of confluence does help here. Two voices in dialogue start out separately in silence, but in dialogue their words and ideas come together, setting off a heuristic turbulence, blending together yet remaining different. Even at its best, when we have the trust, freedom, and openness we have talked about previously, our improvisation is messy.

Implicit in the concept of dialogue, and problematizing it, is the presence of diversity. All individuals exhibit diversity, for each of us is unique in genetics and background; as Myers and Anderson explain, "*Diversity* describes the joining of individuals who differ in cultural, demographic, and cognitive backgrounds." When such individuals are in conversation, when there is dialogue, when there is the improvisation of the soloist working with the band, there is always the reality of difference. When I speak with someone, I realize that that person is not me, does not have my ideas, my dispositions, my background, my words. Consciously or unconsciously I recognize the dynamic of diversity at work in our communicating.

One goal of dialogue is to bring diverse individuals closer together. One of the ways is to be transparent, willing to be vulnerable, for this can assist communication. When this is multiplied within intentional small group gatherings—whether as committees, learning communities, neighborhood meetings, or book clubs—relational elements allow groups to pursue a flow of meaning. Admittedly, pursuing self-understanding involves risks, for in making ourselves transparent we open ourselves to the judgment of others. Nevertheless, without transparency we lose the challenge of connecting our differentiations. The question, then, is this: can we accept the differences generously by listening empathetically?

*Finding out about one's past and future dialectically becomes an active eye into an individual.*

What we reveal and how we bring out selected elements about ourselves can either develop closeness or create distance. Let's say a person describes herself by saying, "I am female, black, young, middle-class, professional, and Canadian." These terms serve to help us understand *what* that person is, but they do not necessarily get at *who* that person is. Defining ourselves by differences, identifying classifications and categories of distinct elements, helps people to know us by contrast to others. But it is our individual narratives that help us and others understand more clearly our inner reality, for narrative deals with causation, motive, values, and change. Learning what another person has done and is striving to do gets at another person's heart. Finding out about one's past and future dialectically becomes an active eye into an individual.

Story is often the way in which the culture or community defines itself. Peter J. Paris shares that in many African cultures music exists for the sake of community. Communication in music takes place in order to define and perpetuate the communal culture. Thus, the soloist is a key cultural figure, for he or she "tells the story of the community while telling his or her own story and by telling it in such a way that his or her unique individuality becomes evident" and the listeners are able to identify that individual, thus sustaining the purpose of community. When we hear a person's story, the facts may be unique, but the revelation of the human condition contains universal elements. This provides cohesiveness among listeners to the stories of individuals.

We are able to relate, to gather, to seek meaning, and to do so in civil ways through dialogue because it is modeled by the Infinite. Irv Brendlinger articulates this trinitarian function: "From eternity the three Persons of the Trinity, the Father, Son, and Holy Spirit co-exist. They live in unity and harmony. They live in eternal conversation or dialogue, and they live in self-giving love to each other." As Sharon Daloz Parks says, "A worthy faith must bear the test of lived experience in the real world—our discoveries and disappointments, expectations and betrayals, assumptions and surprises. It is in the ongoing dialogue between self and world, between community and lived reality, that meaning—a faith—takes form."

*Our willingness to listen with faith, as a child rather than as an expert, grants many more possibilities for dialogue.*

Including faith with dialogue advances the likelihood of relationship. Our willingness to listen with faith, as a child rather than as an expert, grants many more possibilities for dialogue. It may seem a waste of time, especially when you think you know everything about everyone, but we do not know everything. There might seem to be nothing new "under the sun," yet we must admit there are surprises available "under the sun." Ecclesiastes 1:13-14 states this poetically: "I applied my mind to study and to explore by wisdom all that is done under the heavens. What a heavy burden God has laid on humankind! I have seen all the things that are done under the sun; all of them are meaningless, a chasing after the wind." We may want to think we know sufficiently for the sake of security or a bolstered ego, yet in reality we grow to realize how little we know. Dialogue with others can be life-giving.

Debate, on the other hand, implies a lack of faith in the other person. Religious totalitarians typically have a strong conviction that their interpretations of their particular belief systems are legitimate, thereby implying that other religions or other interpretations of the same religions should be condemned. Having strong faith convictions, and even sharing them passionately, is fine, but to force those ideas on others is not. When faith is shared dialogically it builds community, for there is a feeling of unity. Dialogue creates a bond within its relationality.

Dialectical elements found in faith and in improvisation are also found in dialogue. In all three themes—faith, improvisation, dialogue— there is the essential element of free play done in the context of safety and freedom. That dialectic manifests itself in many areas of our existence. Hackney notes that dynamic at work in American history: "This dialogic relationship between individualism and community is one of the main themes of American history. It is not really a tension because Americans in public opinion polls express the same level of enthusiasm for the notion of individualism as for community. Yet it seems paradoxical that we live utterly alone, but have no meaning, no identity, apart from the social context in which we are embedded. It is this twoness in our natures that makes us long for 'community'."

In other contexts—for example jazz, theatre, and basketball—the individual functioning within a group develops trust in himself and the others. It's not only about the skill or creativity of any one person, but rather how the whole group makes it happen. Jazz performers, for example, take turns as individuals as they improvise in their own ways, yet they are being influenced by the others. The same is true in group dialogue. One is speaking, but because that person undoubtedly is aware of the listeners, he or she is somewhat influenced by their presence. And when a newcomer wedges into an established group, though it may be somewhat uncomfortable, it forces everyone to invest even more in order to keep harmony and propel ongoing movement.

Montgomery and Baxter express the path of connectedness rather than control: "Jazz has much in common with our notions about dialectics. Jazz musicians have open invitations to 'sit in on a gig,' to lend their unique vocal and instrumental sounds to the event, and they readily encourage each other to stretch their musical contributions beyond the givens to the potentials of the moment. Collaboration is in the service of spontaneous creativity." The musician must have sufficient confidence and faith in his or her preparation for the gig. When you walk into a foreign situation—for example, a band you've never met—and intentionally remove your defenses, you make yourself vulnerable. This is faith. This is improvisation. This is what is needed for dialogue. There is no guarantee of the outcome; you must be willing to be surprised but have enough faith that the path will unfold. If you are too obsessed with the outcome, you will want to control. If you can bask in the relationships made possible through "stretching," the rewards bring satisfaction.

*Confluence involves the meeting of polarities, and how that messy aggregation is accomplished is mysterious and paradoxical.*

Confluence involves the meeting of polarities, and how that messy aggregation is accomplished is mysterious and paradoxical. The rational supposition would be that the stronger polarity eventually overcomes the weaker, that one is right and the other is wrong. Such a dualistic assumption is limiting. One can see a possible solution in the field of quantum physics. Krista Tippett discusses this in the context of the theory of the nature of light: ". . . consider this: a scientific puzzle that Einstein chewed on, the question of whether light is a particle or a wave, was resolved by a teacher of John Polkinghorne, Paul Dirac, with the unexpected, seemingly illogical conclusion that it is both. And here's the key that made that discovery possible: how we ask our questions affects the answers we arrive at. Light appears as a wave if you ask it 'a wavelike question' and it appears as a particle if you ask it 'a particle-like question.' This is a wonderful template for understanding how contradictory explanations of reality can simultaneously be true."

The framing of questions is significant. "When did you stop beating your wife?" places the listener in a cage full of implications. Searching for truth with accompanying context produces quite a different journey than, say, memorizing facts without any background or surrounding information.

Considering this matter of contexts and connections from the outlook of neuroscience, Iain McGilchrist says, ". . . the right hemisphere pays attention to the Other, whatever it is that exists apart from ourselves, with which it sees itself in profound relation. It is deeply attracted to, and given life by, the relationship, the betweenness, that exists with this Other. By contrast, the left hemisphere pays attention to the virtual world that it has created, which is self-consistent, but self-contained, ultimately disconnected from the Other, making it powerful, but ultimately only able to operate on, and to know, itself." We are made to connect. We do have fears that sometimes prevent social connectedness, but in the long run confronting those fears is worth the price. Developing trust in the Other takes time.

When that trust is achieved, however, we find ourselves on the road to confluence, to dialogue, to discovery. That is the path I have been exploring in the previous chapters.

One teacher told me that there are two reasons we write: first to discover what we think and then to communicate what we have discovered. I have been sharing what I think, what I have discovered. The chart below presents what I see to be the two strands leading to confluence:

| Structure | Freedom |
|---|---|
| Rationality | Intuition |
| Certainty | Unpredictability |
| Control | Surrender |
| Autonomy | Interdependence |
| Singularity | Plurality |
| Debate | Dialogue |

The two lists need each other and need to be in dialogue. Structure is required in order to do anything with Freedom. Instead of approaching life with only Rationality, we can also, not instead, approach life through Intuition. Certainty and Unpredictability pertain to Structure and Freedom, and, as Rationality has to do with Structure, Intuition is an expression of Freedom. The enemy of faith, improvisation, and dialogue is Control, while Surrender ignites all three. The temptation to be in the driver's seat and make decisions with Autonomy can be rectified through Interdependence, a much more socially connective means. Having one and only one view to persuasively prove to others speaks of Singularity. By taking into account other ideas and minimally enjoining others in spirit demonstrates Plurality. The win-lose of Debate as well as the right-wrong element is so thoroughly different from the exploratory mode of Dialogue.

Finding such parallels in faith, improvisation, and dialogue brings added strength to each theme while at the same time building the trilogy. In this rendering of the three practices, faith is the pebble in the pond. I must always remind myself of the power of "structure," that into which I lean (faith), be it Deity, air, an institution, family, a chord chart, a basketball team, or people in general for the sake of improvisation or dialogue. Faith, improvisation, dialogue—they are friends, and they are our friends.

# Questions for Thought
# and Discussion

# Notes

**Chapter One:** *My Relational Faith Journey*

1. What is the first thought that comes to you when you think of the word "faith"? What people come to mind?
2. Where does faith come from?
3. Socrates said the "the unexamined life is not worth living." What value might there be in examining your faith?
4. Must faith always be religious?
5. Describe experiences, both positive and negative, you have had with "people of faith."
6. In what area of your life is faith most active?
7. "Does one believe in order to fulfill an underlying psychological need for love or in order to develop business contacts and professional associates? Does another deny God because a father is distant and aloof or because personal habits do not accord with religious tenets?" (Ruth A. Tucker, *Walking Away from Faith*) Tucker raises the question of why people have faith and notes some possibilities. Why do you or do you not have faith?
8. Is a person born with faith or is faith a result of one's upbringing?
9. What is the role of community in faith?
10. Can I place faith in myself? In others?
11. Can a person have fear and faith at the same time, or are these two concepts mutually exclusive?
12. What is the relationship between confidence and faith?
13. How is faith related to hope? to love?
14. Tell a story from your own life that illustrates how your faith (religious or otherwise) functions.
15. How is faith important in the twenty-first century?

Notes

## Chapter Two: *What Faith Is and Is Not*

1. How are faith and doubt related?
2. How are faith and logic related? In what ways might faith be "crazy"? (Susan W. Smith)
3. In what ways is faith childlike (as opposed to childish)?
4. "Belief is a term associated with faith, but it is not in itself faith." How are faith and belief similar? different?
5. Sharon Daloz Parks said, "Faith is intimately related to doing. . . . Our faith is revealed in our behavior." James 2:26 says, "For just as the body without the spirit is dead, so faith without works is also dead."
   To what extent do you think that faith must be realized in actions?
6. "Once [the tightrope walker] takes his first step, that act of faith leads him into the encounter with risk, fear, and courage."
   How do you experience faith taking you into an encounter with risk, fear, and/or courage?
7. "Faith has much to do with our core values, those things we believe in most deeply, that we see to be good, that give meaning to our lives."
   What are three of your core values? In what ways do they "give meaning" to your life?
8. Have you experienced some form of Coren's "stillness" when making a leaping decision to "go for it"? If so, how was it significant for you? If not, what do you imagine it would look like if you were to experience it?
9. In what ways might faith provide freedom and space for thinking and questioning? Can you give an example from your own experience when this was true?
10. Alberto Salazar said that "everything that happens has a purpose." Do you agree or disagree? Why?
11. How has faith changed you? Can you tell a story that illustrates that change?

Notes

1. In what ways are the terms "belief" and "trust" related to faith?
2. In what ways might a glib repetition of untested belief systems get in the way of real faith?
3. "Faith in something important no doubt has significant value for your life; therefore, to lose such faith jostles your sense of meaning and purpose."
   Describe a time you have experienced this.
4. In what ways might having control be both a blessing and a curse?
5. What fears weaken your faith?
6. How might letting go and living a life of faith help a person construct meaning?
7. "Gracious uncertainty. Breathless expectation. Surprises. These are indeed what we experience in the confluences of life."
   How have any of these been part of your experience?
8. "Common to all religious faiths is the virtue of compassion. The other factors that separate them are overcome by this singular unity."
   Do you agree or disagree? Why?
9. How does the metaphor of confluence help you think about matters of faith?
10. On his radio show Edward R. Murrow used to have a five-minute segment called "This I Believe." Individuals indicated what motivated them or what gave a central focus to their lives.
    In a few sentences, finish this statement: "This I believe . . ."

Notes

## Chapter Four: *My Relational Improvisation Journey*

1. What comes to mind when you hear the word "improvise"?
2. What passion or interest captivated you as a child?
3. When have you experienced someone discouraging or stifling one of your passions or interests?
4. How have your early interests manifested themselves in your life today?
5. "To live by following the script alone is to live partially . . ." How have you found freedom and joy in your life by not always "following the script"?
6. What could you do to encourage the dreams and interests of another?
7. Where have you experienced the "freedom of improvisation and the bondage of perfectionism"?
8. What would you like to *do* with your life that you aren't doing now?
9. What will it take to move in the direction of your dreams?
10. Describe a time when freedom exerted within limitations produced meaning in your life.
11. What is the greatest adventure you have had in your life to this point?
12. What adventure would you like next in your life?

Notes

**Chapter Five:** *What Improvisation Is And Is Not*

1. In your daily life, how do you experience bondage?
2. Share several ways you improvised in your daily activities this past week.
3. Describe a time when you found yourself "lost in the moment."
4. What significance do you find in the observation that "we cannot get away from ourselves"?
5. This chapter talks about the relationship between preparation and improvisation. As you look back on your life, what kinds of preparation have aided your future improvisation?
6. Describe a time when improvising led to discovery.
7. Steve Lacy said that he was attracted to improvisation because it was about "always being on the brink of the unknown and being prepared for the leap."
   How do you feel when you are standing on the brink?
8. In what ways has fear of failure ever been a part of your experience?
9. Describe a situation in which you acted spontaneously.
10. What relationship do you see between the terms in the following pairs:
    creativity and constraints?
    collaboration and improvisation?
    confidence and creativity?
11. How are the world of dreams and the world of creativity related?
12. In your daily life how do you experience freedom?

Notes

1.  In what areas of your life do you feel you have control?
2.  "Control and certainty can blind us to creative, even redemptive, possibilities in the world around us."
    Discuss.
3.  In what ways do you experience this paradox: "Improvisation requires control and simultaneously requires release of control."?
4.  In what ways do you find yourself categorizing people?
5.  The example of looking at Mt. Hood from different positions suggested the benefits of multiple perspectives. How would you benefit from being open to seeing your world from many points of view?
6.  "With too little judgment, we get trash. With too much judgment, we get blockage. In order to play freely, we must disappear. In order to play freely, we must have a command of technique. Back and forth flows the dialogue of imagination and discipline, passion and precision. We harmonize groundedness in daily practice with spiritedness in daily stepping out into the unknown."
    What in your experience enables you to "play freely"?
7.  Give an example of when you have experienced the "fascinating dialectic of structure and freedom."
8.  Describe an experience when you learned from a failure.
9.  "We know that the childlike state allows the combination of both perfection and imperfection."
    Discuss.
10. As Eric Alexander recognized that all humans are fallible and limited, how do you deal with being imperfect?
11. In what area of your life would you like to improvise more?
12. How are faith and improvisation similar?

Notes

**Chapter Seven:** *My Relational Dialogue Journey*

1. Think back to a time when you felt like a misfit. How did you feel? What caused your reactions?
2. Think back to a time when you felt you had no voice. What produced those feelings in you?
3. When did you find your voice? How did you find it?
4. What produces in you a sense of "safety"?
5. "True dialogue . . . develops trust, a trust that is essential to the development of the individual and the group."
   How have you experienced this kind of dialogue?
6. Think of a time when those around you were accepting and non-judgmental. How did you respond to their attitudes?
7. "He [Don Alexander] had many times before asked me, 'What do *you* want to do?'"
   What keeps you from doing what you want to do? What frees you to do what *you* want to do?

Notes

## Chapter Eight: *What Dialogue Is and Is Not*

1. Think back to a time when in a conversation with someone you were able be honest and real. What was that like?
2. What is it about childhood games that is so appealing, even to adults?
3. What about conversation do you most enjoy, most value? Why?
4. When has a conversation changed your life (for good or bad)?
5. Before you read this book, how did you distinguish between conversation and dialogue? How, if at all, have your ideas changed?
6. Share a time when you entered the world of the Other.
7. Describe a time when understanding another's point of view changed you.
8. The chapter distinguishes between dialogue and "pseudo-dialogue." Have you experienced each? If so, how did your feelings and responses differ with each?
9. If you were to be the leader in a group dialogue, what could you do to enhance the process?
10. Mark Gerzon distinguishes between debate and dialogue. When might you choose debate as the more effective approach and when might you prefer dialogue as the better means?
11. What do you perceive to be the advantages of homogeneity and heterogeneity? Which do you tend towards?
12. What are the positive results that come from suspending judgment?
13. Share an experience where collaboration (working together) produced a result superior to that which might have come as a result of working alone.

# Notes

## Chapter Nine: *Dialogue As Confluence*

1. So, can you share other Ole/Lena jokes?
2. "The history of the universe is not the performance of a fixed score, written by God in eternity and inexorably performed by creatures, but it is a grand improvisation in which the Creator and creatures cooperate in the unfolding development of the grand fugue of creation." (John Polkinghorne and Nicholas Beale, *Questions of Truth*)
   What would it mean for you to see God as an improviser? What would it mean for you to see yourself as a co-improviser with God?
3. "Dialogue with others can be life-giving. Debate, on the other hand, implies a lack of faith in the other person."
   Discuss.
4. In your experience, what facilitates and what hinders good communication?
5. What does it mean to listen empathetically?
6. What is important for you to reveal in the telling of your story?
7. "In other contexts—for example jazz, theatre, and basketball—the individual functioning within a group develops trust in himself and the others."
   What other examples would you add to the list and why?
8. In what ways do you experience the dialectic of autonomy versus interdependence?
9. How do you handle the "messy congregation" of confluence in your daily experience?
10. Look again at the chart at the end of the chapter. How do the terms in each of the columns relate to each other? How are the two columns interrelated? How do the terms in the chart manifest themselves in your life?
11. "Faith, improvisation, dialogue—they are friends."
    Discuss.
12. How have you been changed by reading this book?

# Notes

This is not a "scholarly" book and is not intended for an academic audience. Consequently, I have not inserted footnotes in the narrative. Still, some may wish to pursue some of these ideas or to contextualize references. To that end, I have provided here chapter bibliographies of the sources I have used. I encourage you to pursue any or all of these; they have meant much to me and I hope they can be enlivening for you.

Now, a word about citations from the Bible. I have used a number of translations throughout this book. All translations bring out only part of the original. I encourage you to use your own version; better yet, look at a number of versions, both to get nuances and to see contexts.

# Works Cited

**CHAPTER ONE**

Daniel Taylor
*The Myth of Certainty: The Reflective Christian & the Risk of Commitment*
Intervarsity Press, Downers Grove, IL (1992)

Irv Brendlinger
*The Call to Authenticity, A Handbook of Hope for the Church*
Emeth Press, Lexington, KY (2009)

Nels F. S. Ferré
*Know Your Faith*
Harper & Brothers, N.Y. (1959)

Reinhold Niebuhr
*The Irony of American History*
The U of Chicago P (1952; 2008)

Carol Gilligan
*In a Different Voice*
Harvard UP, Cambridge (1982/1993)

Sharon Daloz Parks
*Big Questions, Worthy Dreams: Mentoring Young Adults in Their Search for Meaning, Purpose, and Faith*
Jossey-Bass, San Francisco (2000)

Donald McCullough
*The Consolations of Imperfection: Learning to Appreciate Life's Limitations*
Brazos, Grand Rapids, MI (2004)

Parker J. Palmer
*The Promise of Paradox: A Celebration*
Ave Maria Press, Notre Dame (1980)

Mark Labberton
*The Dangerous Act of Worship: Living God's Call to Justice*
Intervarsity Press, Downers Grove, IL (2007)

James W. Fowler
*Stages of Faith: The Psychology of Human Development and the Quest for Meaning*
HarperCollins, N.Y. (1981)

**CHAPTER TWO**

Paul Tillich
*Dynamics of Faith*
Harper & Row, N.Y. (1957)

Scott Russell Sanders
*Hunting for Hope: A Father's Journeys*
Beacon Press, Boston (1998)

Frederich Buechner
*Secrets in the Dark: A Life in Sermons*
HarperCollins, San Francisco (2006)

Gregory A. Boyd
*The Myth of a Christian Religion*
Zondervan, Grand Rapids, MI (2009)

Philip Yancey
*Reaching for the Invisible God*
Zondervan, Grand Rapids, MI (2000)

John Tarrant
*The Light Inside the Dark: Zen, Soul, and the Spiritual Life*
HarperCollins, N.Y. (1998)

Sharon Daloz Parks
*Big Questions, Worthy Dreams: Mentoring Young Adults in Their Search for Meaning, Purpose, and Faith*
Jossey-Bass, San Francisco (2000)

Anna Halpin in Ch. 4 "The Process Is the Purpose"
Frank Barron, Alfonso Montuori and Anthea Barron, eds.
*Creators on Creating: Awakening and Cultivating the Imaginative Mind*
Tarcher/Penguin, N.Y. (1997)

Susan K. Williams Smith
*Crazy Faith: Ordinary People, Extraordinary Lives*
Judson Press, Valley Forge, PA (2009)

Klyne Snodgrass
*The NIV Application Commentary, Ephesians*
Zondervan, Grand Rapids, MI (1996)

Alberto Salazar & John Brant
*14 Minutes: A Running Legend's Life and Death and Life*
Rodale, N.Y. (2012)

## CHAPTER THREE

Marcus Borg
*Speaking Christian: Why Christian Words Have Lost Their Meaning and Power—and How They Can Be Restored*
HarperCollins, N.Y. (2011)

Ron Martoia
*The Bible as Improv: Seeing & Living the Script in New Ways*
Zondervan, Grand Rapids, MI (2010)

Alzina Stone Dale
*The Outline of Sanity: A Biography of G. K. Chesterton*
Eerdmans, Grand Rapids, MI (1982)

James E. Loder and W. Jim Neidhardt
*The Knight's Move: The Relational Logic of the Spirit in Theology and Science*
Helmers & Howard, Colorado Springs, CO (1992)

Oswald Chambers
*My Utmost for His Highest* (April 29th "The Graciousness of Uncertainty")
Dodd, Mead & Company, N.Y. (1959)

Philip Yancey
*Reaching for the Invisible God*
Zondervan, Grand Rapids, MI (2000)

Leonard Susskind
*The Black Hole War: My Battle with Stephen Hawking To Make the World Safe for Quantum Mechanics*
Little, Brown and Company, N.Y. (2008)

Eric Liu
*Guiding Lights: The People Who Lead Us Toward Our Purpose in Life*
Ballantine Books, N.Y. (2004)

Gregory Bateson
*Steps to an Ecology of Mind*
Ballantine, N.Y. (1972)

Donald McCullough
*The Consolations of Imperfection: Learning to Appreciate Life's Limitations*
Brazos, Grand Rapids, MI (2004)

Terry Eagleton
*The Meaning of Life*
Oxford UP, N.Y. (2007)

Kathleen Norris
*Amazing Grace: A Vocabulary of Faith*
Riverhead Books, N.Y. (1998)

Susan K. Williams Smith
*Crazy Faith: Ordinary People, Extraordinary Lives*
Judson Press, Valley Forge, PA (2009)

Juan Williams & Quinton Dixie
*This Far by Faith: Stories from the African American Religious Experience*
HarperCollins, N.Y. (2003)

C. S. Lewis
*Mere Christianity*
Macmillan, N.Y. (1943)

Annie Dillard
*Holy the Firm*
Harper & Row, N.Y. (1977)

**CHAPTER FOUR**

Alan P. Merriam
*The Anthropology of Music*
Northwestern UP, Evanston, IL (1964)

Randy Halberstadt
*Metaphors for the Musician: Perspectives from a Jazz Pianist*
Sher Music Co., Petaluma, CA (2001)

Colleen Shaddox in
Jay Allison and Dan Gediman, ed.
*This I Believe: The Personal Philosophies of Remarkable Men and Women*
Henry Holt, N.Y. (2006)

**CHAPTER FIVE**

Daniel J. Wiener
*Rehearsals for Growth: Theater Improvisation for Psychotherapists*
Norton, N.Y. (1994)

Jon Kabat-Zinn
*Wherever You Go, There You Are: Mindfulness Meditation in Everyday Life*
Hyperion, N.Y. (2005)

Steve Lacy in
Derek Bailey
*Improvisation: Its Nature and Practice In Music*
Da Capo Press, N.Y. 1992

Wynton Marsalis with Geoffrey C. Ward
*Moving to Higher Ground: How Jazz Can Change Your Life*
Random House, N.Y. (2008)

Eric Liu
*Guiding Lights: The People Who Lead Us Toward Our Purpose in Life*
Ballantine Books, N.Y. (2004)

Lloyd Peterson
*Music and the Creative Spirit: Innovators in Jazz, Improvisation, and the Avant Garde*
Studies in Jazz, No. 52
Scarecrow Press, Lanham, MD (2006)

Sally Schneider
*The Improvisational Cook*
HarperCollins, N.Y. (2006)

Kareem Abdul-Jabbar
*On the Shoulders of Giants: My Journey Through the Harlem Renaissance*
Simon & Schuster, N.Y. (2007)

Alan Arkin
*An Improvised Life: A Memoir*
Da Capo Press, Cambridge (2011)

**CHAPTER SIX**

Iain McGilchrist
*The Master and His Emissary: The Divided Brain and the Making of the Western World*
Yale UP, New Haven (2009)

Will Earhart in
Henry Martin
*Enjoying Jazz*
Schirmer, N.Y. (1986)

James E. Loder and W. Jim Neidhardt
*The Knight's Move: The Relational Logic of the Spirit in Theology and Science*
Helmers & Howard, Colorado Springs, CO (1992)

Mary Crossan and Marc Sorrenti in
Ken N. Kamoche; Miguel Pina e Cunha; Joao Viera da Cunha, ed.
*Organizational Improvisation*
Routledge, N.Y. (2002)

Keith Sawyer
*Group Genius: The Creative Power of Collaboration*
Basic Books, N.Y. (2007)

Richard Farson and Ralph Keyes
*Whoever Makes the Most Mistakes Wins: The Paradox of Innovation*
The Free Press, N.Y. (2002)

Jay Phelan
*The Covenant Companion*, p. 5, June 2009

Howard Gardner
*Five Minds for the Future*
Harvard Business School Press, Boston (2006)

Crockett Johnson
*Harold and the Purple Crayon*
Scholastic, N.Y. (1955)

Stephen Nachmanovitch
*Free Play: The Power of Improvisation in Life and the Arts*
G. P. Putnam's Sons, N.Y. (1990)

Eric Alexander: Nightlife in Tokyo, CD
Liner notes, Ted Panken
Milestone Records MCD-9330-2, Berkeley (2003)

Eric Barnhill
Facts About Improvisation, February 24, 2006 from The Daily
Improvisation
http://ericbarnhill.wordpress.com/facts-about-improvisation/

Lou Antolihao
*Culture of Improvisation: Informal Settlements and Slum Upgrading in a
Metro Manila Locality*
Institute of Philippine Culture, Ateneo de Manila University, Quezon
City (2004)

Peter J. Paris
*The Spirituality of African Peoples: The Search for a Common Moral
Discourse*
Fortress Press, Minneapolis (1995)

Mary Catherine Bateson
*Composing a Life*
Grove Press, N.Y. (1989)

Byron Kirk Jones
Quoted in film *Sonny Rollins: Saxophone Colossus*, 1986
*The Jazz of Preaching: How to Preach with Great Freedom and Joy*
Abingdon, Nashville, TN (2004)

Ben Ratliff
*The Jazz Ear: Conversations Over Music*
Henry Holt, N.Y. (2008)

Fred Frith in
Lloyd Peterson
*Music and the Creative Spirit: Innovators in Jazz, Improvisation, and the Avant Garde*
Studies in Jazz, No. 52
The Scarecrow Press, Inc., Lanham, MD (2006)

Cornel West
*Race Matters*
Vintage Books, N.Y. (1994)

Frank J. Barrett
Ch. 7 "Creativity and improvisation in jazz and organizations: Implications for organizational learning" in
Ken N. Kamoche; Miguel Pina e Cunha; Joao Viera da Cunha, ed.
*Organizational Improvisation*
Routledge, N.Y. (2002)

Paul F. Berliner
"Art Farmer On Jazz Learning and Improvisation"
*Jazzforschung/Jazz Research*, Volume 39 (December, 2007)

Dorothy Leeds
*The 7 Powers of Questions: Secrets to Successful Communication in Life and at Work*
Penguin Putnam, N.Y. (2000)

Constantin Stanislavski
*An Actor Prepares*
Trans. Elizabeth Reynolds Hapgood
Theatre Arts, (1936)/Routledge, N.Y. (1989)

Paul F. Berliner
*Thinking in Jazz: The Infinite Art of Improvisation*
The U of Chicago P (1994)

Carol S. Goul and Kenneth Keaton
"The Essential Role of Improvisation in Musical Performance"
*Journal of Art and Art Criticism*, 58:2 (Spring 2000)

## CHAPTER SEVEN

Wynton Marsalis with Geoffrey C. Ward
*Moving to Higher Ground: How Jazz Can Change Your Life*
Random House, N.Y. (2008)

Martha C. Nussbaum
*Cultivating Humanity: A Classical Defense of Reform in Liberal Education*
Harvard UP, Cambridge (1997)

## CHAPTER EIGHT

Susan Scott
*Fierce Conversations: Achieving Success at Work & in Life, One Conversation at a Time*
Viking Penguin, N.Y. (2002)

Juanita Brown with David Isaacs
*The World Café: Shaping Our Futures Through Conversations That Matter*
Berrett-Koehler, San Francisco (2005)

Preben Friis, "Presence and spontaneity in improvisational work"
*Experiencing Risk, Spontaneity and Improvisation in Organizational Change: Working Live*
Patricia Shaw and Ralph Stacey, ed.
Routledge, London (2006)

Erving Goffman
*Frame Analysis: An Essay on the Organization of Experience*
Harper & Row, N.Y. (1974)

Theodore Zeldin
*Conversation: How Talk Can Challenge Our Lives*
Hidden Spring, Mahwah, NJ (2000)

Keith Sawyer
*Group Genius: The Creative Power of Collaboration*
Basic Books, N.Y. (2007)

Jerome Bruner
*Actual Minds, Possible Worlds*
Harvard UP, Cambridge (1986)

Peter M. Senge
*The Fifth Discipline: The Art and Practice of the Learning Organization*
Doubleday, N.Y. (1990)

George Kunz
*The Paradox of Power and Weakness: Levinas and an Alternative Paradigm*
State University of New York P, Albany (1998)

Deborah L. Flick
*From Debate To Dialogue: Using the Understanding Process to Transform Our Conversations*
Orchid Publications, Boulder, CO (1998)

Cynthia Barton Rabe
*The Innovation Killer: How What We Know Limits What We Can Imagine –*
*And What Smart Companies Are Doing About It*
Amacom, N.Y. (2006)

Sharon Daloz Parks
*Big Questions, Worthy Dreams: Mentoring Young Adults in Their Search*
*for Meaning, Purpose, and Faith*
Jossey-Bass, San Francisco (2000)

David Richo
*How To Be an Adult in Relationships: The Five Keys to Mindful Loving*
Shambhala, Boston (2002)

David Bohm
*On Dialogue*
Routledge, N.Y. (1996)

Arnold Mindell
*The Leader as Martial Artist: An Introduction to Deep Democracy*
Lao Tse Press, Portland, OR (2000)

Parker J. Palmer
*A Hidden Wholeness: The Journey Toward an Undivided Life*
Jossey-Bass, San Francisco (2004)

David Borgo
*Sync Or Swarm: Improvising Music in a Complex Age*
Continuum, N.Y. (2005)

Mark Gerzon
*Leading Through Conflict: How Successful Leaders Transform Differences*
*into Opportunities*
Harvard Business School P, Boston (2006)

Daniel Yankelovich
*The Magic of Dialogue: Transforming Conflict into Cooperation*
Simon & Schuster, N.Y. (1999)

**CHAPTER NINE**

Scott A. Myers and Carolyn M. Anderson
*The Fundamentals of Small Group Communication*
Sage Publications, Thousand Oaks, CA (2008)

Peter J. Paris
*The Spirituality of African Peoples: The Search for a Common Moral Discourse*
Fortress Press, Minneapolis, MN (1995)

Irv Brendlinger
*The Call to Authenticity: A Handbook of Hope for the Church*
Emeth Press, Lexington, KY (2009)

Sharon Daloz Parks
*Big Questions, Worthy Dreams: Mentoring Young Adults in Their Search for Meaning, Purpose, and Faith*
Jossey-Bass, San Francisco (2000)

Sheldon Hackney, "Shades of Freedom in America"
*Freedom: Reassessments and Rephrasings*
Jose V. Ciprut, ed.
The MIT Press, Cambridge (2008)

Barbara M. Montgomery and Leslie A. Baxter in
*Dialectical Approaches to Studying Personal Relationships*
Barbara M. Montgomery, ed.
Lawrence Erlbaum, Mahwah, NJ (1998)

Krista Tippett
*Speaking of Faith*
Viking, N.Y. (2007)

Iain McGilchrist
*The Master and His Emissary: The Divided Brain and the Making of the Western World*
Yale UP, New Haven (2009)

## OTHER SOURCES THAT INFORMED AND INSPIRED

Robert Gelinas
*Finding the Groove: Composing a Jazz-Shaped Faith*
Zondervan, Grand Rapids, MI (2009)

Paul Haidet
"Jazz and the 'Art' of Medicine: Improvisation in the Medical Encounter"
Annals of Family Medicine, Vol. 5 No. 2 March/April 2007

Doug Pagitt
*Preaching Re-Imagined: The Role of the Sermon in Communities of Faith*
Zondervan, Grand Rapids, MI (2005)

R. Keith Sawyer, ed.
*Structure and Improvisation in Creative Teaching*
Cambridge UP, N.Y. (2011)

Twyla Tharp
*The Collaborative Habit: Life Lessons for Working Together*
Simon & Schuster, N.Y. (2009)

Karl E. Weick and Kathleen M. Sutcliffe
*Managing the Unexpected: Assuring High Performance in an Age of Complexity*
Jossey-Bass, San Francisco (2001)

Samuel Wells
*Improvisation: The Drama of Christian Ethics*
Brazos, Grand Rapids, MI (2004)

16249817R00107

Made in the USA
San Bernardino, CA
25 October 2014